BLAKE SHELTON

BLAKE SHELTON
HAPPY ANYWHERE

CAROL CASH LARGE

Backbeat
Books
Guilford, Connecticut

Backbeat
Books

An imprint of Globe Pequot, the trade division of The Rowman & Littlefield
Publishing Group, Inc.
4501 Forbes Blvd., Ste. 200
Lanham, MD 20706
www.rowman.com

Distributed by NATIONAL BOOK NETWORK

Library of Congress Cataloging-in-Publication Data available

Names: Large, Carol Cash, author.
Title: Blake Shelton : happy anywhere / Carol Cash Large.
Description: Lanham : Backbeat, 2022. | Includes index.
Identifiers: LCCN 2021049716 (print) | LCCN 2021049717 (ebook) | ISBN
    9781493065202 (cloth) | ISBN 9781493065219 (epub)
Subjects: LCSH: Shelton, Blake. | Country musicians—United
    States—Biography. | LCGFT: Biographies.
Classification: LCC ML420.S53645 L37 2022 (print) | LCC ML420.S53645
    (ebook) | DDC 782.421642092 [B]—dc23
LC record available at https://lccn.loc.gov/2021049716
LC ebook record available at https://lccn.loc.gov/2021049717

∞™ The paper used in this publication meets the minimum requirements of
American National Standard for Information Sciences—Permanence of Paper
for Printed Library Materials, ANSI/NISO Z39.48-1992

For Debi and Patti

CONTENTS

FOREWORD

Growing up in Ada, Oklahoma, with absolutely zero connection to the music industry made my dream of making it in country music feel like a crazy fantasy. Luckily for me, as a very young teenager, I met Larry and Carol Large, who also shared the same love for country music as I did!! Even though we really had no clue how I was gonna make it, we all believed somehow, I would. These stories of our journey are directly from Carol's point of view. I wouldn't trade these times in my life for the world and I hope you love Carol and Larry's stories as much as I love Carol and Larry themselves.

I would still be roofing houses in Ada, Oklahoma, without them.

PREFACE

You may ask yourself, "Why did Carol write this book?" I have asked myself that question, and it boils down to the fact that I have always wanted to write a book. I did start one a few times but never had my heart in it. Like I told students for years, write about what you love and know; I finally realized I had a subject others would enjoy that fit those two requirements as well.

I love Blake Shelton. I know Blake Shelton. And about five years ago, I let Blake know that I was seriously considering writing a book about our lives with him. By that time, I had known Blake about twenty-five years. He was just a seventeen-year-old kid when, with his parents' blessings, we moved him to Nashville in 1994, two weeks out of high school. My husband Larry and I both believed he had everything it would take to be successful: dedication, talent, personality, and appearance, in that order. I would later add loyalty because it takes a little bit of time to realize whether or not someone possesses that quality. Blake has it all—and then some!

So, I am presenting a variety of stories and successes—some inspiring, some unusual, but mostly funny—that we experienced with him along the way. I sincerely hope you enjoy reading about the many adventures we have shared over the years.

Oh, and did I say, I love Blake Shelton!

—Carol Cash Large

ACKNOWLEDGMENTS

Carol thanks. . .

Blake Shelton, what a wonderful journey with you—more family than friend * Larry, the social butterfly in our family * Debi, my first daughter and the perfect proofreader for those early drafts * Patti, my last daughter and the one who helped me remember the humor in some of my stories * Shelley Henry, my bonus daughter who is always supportive * Linda McGaha, Anna Cash, Monica Walton, and Mandy Davison who were a part of this endeavor * Connie Schultz, who was Blake's #1 fan and knew more about his professional life than the professionals, Amy Jacobs, Fran Carpenter, Evelyn Martin, Kelli Sampsel, Mike and Angie Stafford * Friends and family who have supported me both through fan club and writing this book, especially Gayle and Megan Sheehan, Farrell and Sue Large, and Gil and Barbara Ragland—couldn't have done it without all of you * Photographers: Anna Orf, Savannah Lutrell, Joe Ownbey, Sherry Urton, Pat Johnson, and Diana Mason Ross * Wes Vause, who aided Blake in proofreading my finished manuscript * Narvel Blackstock, Brandon Blackstock, Dana Kelley Lobb, Berkley Myers, Alissa Endres, and the amazing Kevin Canady for all they did or do to keep us in the loop * Bob Burke for his encouragement * Marilyn Allen, who led me by the hand through this entire process * John Cerullo, for seeing the potential in my book, and the team at Backbeat Books: Chris Chappell, Laurel Myers, Carol Flannery, Barb Claire, Jessica Thwaite, Judith Schnell, Jessica Kastner, James Barnett, and Nancy Bryan * Dorothy Shackleford, Dick Shelton, Endy Intrieri, and the entire Shelton/Byrd families for always supporting Blake * And music, for making everything possible.

PROLOGUE

Ada, Oklahoma! It was a pretty rowdy place back in 1909, and one block in particular (where 38 murders took place in just one year) was known as the "bucket of blood." Men were being killed over property rights, cow thefts, or scornful looks. One notable night, local folk had their fill of some out-of-town scoundrels who were being held in the city jail for murdering a man of the law. As those well-connected criminals were rumored to be living it up in their cell with steak dinners and cozy accoutrements, a couple hundred locals decided they couldn't stomach those obscenities any longer. They stormed the jail very early one morning, took the four accused men to an abandoned livery stable, bound them with baling wire, and lynched them.

Two years before Blake Shelton was born, Welborn Hope published a book, *Four Men Hanging: The End of the Old West*. That documented event later morphed into an interesting slogan: "Ada: A Great Place to Hang Out."

Times gradually changed and the area surrounding Ada was booming during the early oil days. Fittstown, Oil Center, Fitzhugh, and others were having a ride on the black gold roller coaster but in the end, their towns stayed small while Ada continued to grow.

By 1976, Ada had become a cozy little university town where ranchers and oilmen from surrounding areas brought their families to shop or get a haircut, while teenagers chose to drag main (before that tradition bit the dust) or take in a drive-in movie on Saturday night.

East Central University (ECU), located at the far east end of Ada's Main Street, was the hub of the community and the small city's largest employer at that time. However, according to *The Chickasaw Newsletter*, Volume 5, No. 2, 1976, the Chickasaw Nation held a groundbreaking ceremony for their tribal office's move to headquarters in Ada from Tishomingo, with few realizing the importance that held for the community. (Blake would later work with Chickasaw governor Bill Anoatubby in efforts to boost the economy in Tishomingo, Oklahoma.) ECU was primarily a teacher's college and where my husband Larry and I received our degrees in the late 1960s and early 1970s. If you started driving west from there, you would first pass Thompson's Book and Supply Co. and Perry's Laundromat, and then travel only a couple of blocks before crossing Mississippi Avenue to continue down Main.

Ada's Main Street was dotted with mom-and-pop businesses like Folger's Drive-In, which had been around for three decades and was well known for their already legendary hamburgers. Many a day was spent calling in an order upon leaving work so it would be ready and waiting after that long, grueling seven-minute drive to the cafe. There was no need to get out of your car either, because Folger's was equipped with a drive-thru window before drive-thru windows were cool! When the line got too long, an employee or one of the Folgers themselves would simply look outside to see who was there and deliver their order. They would know what you ordered without asking because repeat customers were the norm. With Folger's guiding the way, Ada had more than their fair share of drive-thru windows. Almost every restaurant and gas station in town accommodated customers by serving them as they remained seated in their cars.

Another noteworthy addition on Main was the Julianna Hotel with its colorful history. Situated on the south side of the street, the long-standing rumor that it was a house of ill repute made it a magnet for a good teenage dare. Unfortunately, my daughter Patti was always up for a dare, so naturally she found herself in the lobby of the Julianna one Saturday night. She walked into a dark foyer to see an old black and white console TV playing to one odd man sitting and staring emotionless in front of it. She quickly went up to the counter and approached a woman (who could have been Dolly Parton's prototype for her role in *The Best Little Whorehouse in Texas*) and asked, "May I use the phone?" The woman motioned to a phone at the end of the counter. Patti looked up and saw rooms, some with lights on, some not, made her fake phone call, and high-tailed it out of there, fulfilling her dare.

Continuing down Main past the barber shop with the red and white barber pole were Perry-McGee Furniture, Campbell's Furniture, Anthony's, and Dillon's Department Store, where clerks were obviously paid commission because their employees followed customers around like little puppy dogs, pointing out good buys. The Front Porch was a children's boutique that actually sported a front porch façade welcoming in the fashionable youth whose parents could afford the nicer clothes they stocked. Easter shopping became an annual event there for some moms on a budget and their kiddos. It was exciting to dress up the little ones in a special frock for that occasion, usually complete with a hat, gloves, and a tiny handbag for girls or jacket and tie for boys. Since Ada was located squarely in the middle of the Bible Belt, Easter was a family event if not a full-fledged Easter Parade. Some of my cutest pictures are of daughters, Debi and Patti, all dressed up in their once-a-year outfits.

Older patrons had their favorite spots too. One business savvy gentleman owned two ladies' shops. The Fashion catered to the trendy younger crowd, while more mature women usually preferred The Smart Shop a few doors down. It sported a curved elongated permanent canopy and patrons felt a dignified ambiance immediately upon walking through the door. Purchasing a skirt and sweater or a dress there made for a good day of shopping.

Right next door was Shipe's Shoes, where shoes lined all the walls, top to bottom and in between. They offered Buster Brown shoes for children and were equipped with a small kiddie ride and a state-of-the-art shoe size finder. Shoes for the entire family were available with one quick stop.

And then there was Evans Hardware, where strangely enough, future brides registered for gifts. It was far more than just a hardware store. There was a story that may or may not be true about

Mr. Evans and Coach Elvan George, who was an outstanding football coach in Oklahoma, first at Ada High School and later at East Central University, and considered one of the most influential figures in Oklahoma sports history. It seems Mr. Evans was a big football fan and he would go to practices and give Coach suggestions on who should play or what the play should be, that sort of thing. Coach never said much, but one Saturday he showed up at the hardware store wearing an apron and carrying a feather duster. He started dusting and making suggestions on how the store should be rearranged. Mr. Evans asked what he was doing, to which Coach replied something along the lines of, "Well, I thought if you could tell me how to run my team, I could give you some pointers on how to run your store." According to the story, they had a good laugh and remained friends but the coaching suggestions ended. That could only happen in a small close-knit town like Ada, Oklahoma.

The First National Bank and Gem Credit Jewelers were also easily accessible right there on the main drag.

Crossing Broadway Avenue, still headed west, was Bryan's Corner Drug, that housed a pharmacy, costume jewelry, a makeup counter, and even a lunch counter at the back where junior high kids had standing orders and would manage to walk the few blocks from school, eat, and walk back in about thirty minutes. I don't know how they did it. Located catty-cornered across the street was Starship 10, a sort of nightclub for preteens and teens in the disco years. Patti still has her *Saturday Night Fever* blue satin tennis shoes and is still hoping to get them autographed one day by Mr. John Travolta, whose picture is on the box.

S&Q Clothiers, Black's Men and Boys Wear, and E M Clothiers were conveniently located in the same vicinity to make shopping easy for the guys. Pete Edgar Jewelers and the McSwain Theatre (where Blake would later earn his first $50 for singing), the last of the original four movie theaters still showing current films, were also popular businesses.

In most of the stores, you could open a charge account or at least put things on layaway. Also, it was not uncommon to take things out on approval, where customers were allowed to take outfits home and try them before purchasing—to decide if they really wanted to keep them or take the ones back they didn't want.

The locally owned Katz Department Store was in the next block. Lots of women, myself included, still constructed some of their own clothing and that seemed to be the best place to find quality fabric. Grace George (wife of Coach George) was my clothing instructor in college and she preferred we shop at Katz for our fabric needs.

Two popular restaurants were Ada's favorite greasy spoons: Hamburger King and mom-and-pop business Liberty Café. Walking into the Liberty Café was like taking a trip back in time. There was a table set up in the kitchen and when an older Black gentleman came in to eat, that might be where he went. You see, during segregation, that was where the Black patrons *had* to sit. But, during that shameful time in our history, those segregated men became friends with the cook who was also the owner. Now they didn't have to sit there, but they sometimes chose to so they could have a nice visit with their friend while they ate. He would even cut up the meat for customers if they had a little arthritis in their hands. My father-in-law always headed back there for that extra courtesy. The cook's wife was a unique soul as well. It was not uncommon for a customer to place an order only to receive something not exactly right. If you complained, the common retort from her was, "Are you hungry?" "Well, yes . . . but," "Then you'll eat it!" Locals loved being treated *just* like they were at Grandma's house. It was those quirky little things that made Ada special and home to the fifteen thousand or so that lived there.

Moving on past Rhynes and Rhodes Furniture and Hudson's Furniture to the far west end of Main was (Blake's mom) Dorothy Shelton's hair salon, Beauty Unlimited. From ECU on the east end to Beauty Unlimited on the west end, Main Street was the heart of Ada, but as with any growing town, there was more.

What wasn't located on Main Street could generally be found on Broadway Avenue, which earlier had housed the Round Bale Cotton Gin, saloons, and jail during the rowdy years. At the corner of Main and Broadway, if you turned south, you would find the Aldridge Hotel, Ada Fire Station, Ada City Jail, and numerous protestant churches. If you turned north from there, you would go past the Ada Evening News and Bowie Ballard Ford.

Past the car lots was JD's Café, known for their pies, and Bob's Bar-B-Que, where more than a few famous folks flew into the small airport a little farther north just to try the renowned cuisine. Through town gossip I had heard that it was not always noted for cleanliness—locals would say (tongue in cheek), "I don't care if my BBQ comes with a side of roach, it's just that good!" My Patti loved Bob's! You would also pass the Indian Hills Motel with the two-story dome-shaped restaurant appearing to have hopped out of *The Jetsons*. It looked like it should have rotated, but it didn't. And there was KADA Radio, and the popular Shirt Nook where you could depend on that unique smell from the presses that sealed designs onto the shirts. Almost anything you wanted could be printed on a tee shirt in nice block letters, or your favorite icon could adorn it with a rubbery likeness from those presses. It was a smell you never forgot, like the smell of donuts in a bakery, hot dogs at the state fair, or gasoline at a service station.

Like Broadway, Mississippi ran north and south, the first busy street nearest ECU. Businesses on Mississippi included gas stations, fast food places, and the Village Inn (where Blake would learn to appreciate karaoke). But there were also Forget-Me-Not Florist and Wellington Photography, where, if you could afford it, you got your senior picture made. Marion Fenton was located on South Mississippi, just before you got to the Village Inn. It was there that (Blake's dad) Richard "Dick" Shelton sold cars.

If you headed north on Mississippi and turned right at Ada's famous crazy corner (four-way stop), you would have found yourself on Arlington Street. The We-Pak-Um station on Arlington gave wooden nickels when you bought beer so you could save them and trade them in for more beer. Farther out was KTEN-TV, an affiliate television station that also produced some original programming in its early years. They had the *KTEN Ranch Hands Show* with Rocky Stone, and my husband Larry played drums and sang on that show. Continue down Arlington clear to the edge of town to find Valley View Hospital and the Oak Hills Drive-In movie theater, which was already in decline. It played B movies but the speakers all still worked and the concession stand wasn't half bad.

Southeast of town was Wintersmith Park, with a beautiful lake and walking path, a monkey cage, peacocks, deer, a train ride, slides, a merry-go-round, a softball park, a lodge, picnic tables, a swimming pool, and a beautiful recreational area. P. A. Norris had donated ten acres of land to the city of Ada for a park in 1933. During the depression, young men had been given jobs through the government's CCC program to come to Ada and build the stone buildings, dam, amphitheater, and so forth, and the city continued to improve on it.

Near Stonewall, fourteen miles farther southeast of town was the Ken Lance Sports Arena (where Blake would play in the future), famous for its huge rodeo every year featuring country stars who performed during the event itself and later at a dance. Ken and Ruth Lance had a wooden dance floor and a regular band, the Country Lancers (with Larry as drummer), but during the rodeo you could have caught Willie Nelson, George Jones, Barbara Mandrell, Reba McEntire (who was just beginning her career), and almost every charting singer of the day. It was almost a rite of passage to go to the dance and get to see a fight. The bouncers got them out of the dance hall pretty quickly but fists sometimes flew. Everyone has a story.

Ada, like Mayberry (on steroids), had a very small-town atmosphere. You would run into someone you knew no matter where you went. If you were driving, it was tradition to lift your pointer finger from the wheel as a way to say hello to anyone you met. It was a busy little town, friendly and over an hour from Oklahoma City, a little farther to Tulsa. In fact, no interstate highway ran through Ada (still doesn't). Townspeople referred to Oklahoma City as "the city," the place to shop if you wanted to get something a little different from everyone else. And, except for the annual rodeo, you would have had to drive to the city to see a big concert. Elvis Presley made one of his final stops there in 1977 and I'm happy to say I attended it with my two daughters, Debi and Patti.

Yep, Ada was a typical midwestern town, then and now.

CHAPTER ONE

THE BABY

1976. Six months and eighteen days into the year brought a typically hot, humid, and rainy summertime day in Oklahoma. All across America, everyone was in the midst of planning for the big bicentennial celebrations that were soon to come. Red, white, and blue semicircular buntings were hung from balcony railings and flags were flying in front of almost everyone's home. BBQ party invitations had been mailed and kids were gearing up for a big day. A fireworks stand could be found on almost every corner along with their sparklers, roman candles, and black cats ready to light the night. A huge event was being organized for Wintersmith Park in Ada. Excitement was in the air that day, but it all came to a screeching halt for one family when *Blake Tollison Shelton* decided to make his debut. Parents Dick and Dorothy Shelton and older brother and sister Richie and Endy, along with a passel of extended family members, welcomed the cute little boy with the big dimples and loud voice into their lives with no reason to believe that his would one day become a recognizable name across the nation.

His middle name, Tollison, came from his paternal grandfather, who didn't care for it as a middle name for himself or his grandson, and he later told him just that. His grandpa died when Blake was only nine years old, but he still has his name and the little memory of how he got it from the namesake himself. In a small stroke of genius, Blake would later do something that would guarantee I could never forget his birthday. He added the line "it's been six months and 18 days" into one of his songs.

What I know about Blake's early years comes from memories relayed to me by family and friends. It is obvious from the stories

1

that he hasn't changed a great deal. Even as a baby, Blake often went with his mom to work and quickly learned how to charm women of all ages. How could he miss with those dimples? I have several acquaintances who remember baby Blake hanging out at Beauty Unlimited. They reminisce about playing with him, even helping out by changing his diaper from time to time, and all agree that he was a pleasant child. The shop had a festive atmosphere and one could probably hear Dorothy's hearty infectious one-syllable belly laugh, "*Ha!*" before walking through the door of her popular beauty shop. It was a great place to visit and there were always several women around. One might be getting her hair styled for a Farrah Fawcett or Dolly Parton look, while others chose to emulate America's Sweetheart, Dorothy Hamill, the Olympian figure skater who popularized a short and sassy look that took the country by storm. Others might be under the dryer, waiting a turn, or maybe just hanging out to play with Blake. Known around town as an Ann-Margret look-alike, Dorothy was not only beautiful but fun-loving, creative, and talented as well. Blake undoubtedly picked up those unique qualities from his mom.

Blake's dad Richard Shelton, known to everyone as Dick, was blessed with a colorful vocabulary, good looks, and a friendly demeanor, all combining to make him the perfect salesman. Tall and thin, with plenty of hair which would soon turn totally gray, he was an honest man and almost everyone in Ada has a car story about him, either from buying one or from watching him race his own car. He simply loved cars! If Blake got his gregarious nature and creative talent from his mother, he definitely got his knack for telling a good story and classic good looks from his dad.

The Shelton family lived in Latta, southwest of Ada, and Blake dearly loved the space offered by being a little bit country and thus able to explore the great outdoors. He was drawn to fishing and later to hunting. He talks about those days with affection, how he explored every square inch of the property. He would wander around until his mother called him to the house from the front porch. The earliest pictures of Blake show him pretending to play a guitar, fishing, racing, and boating, all things he still loves today.

Dorothy says he never met a stranger. Everywhere he went, he struck up a conversation with anyone close, young or old. He made friends everywhere he went.

One of my favorite stories his mom shares is when he was four years old and the family was next door at a cookout. After they had grilled and were ready to sit down to eat, not surprisingly, Blake was happily playing with a frog. When she handed him a hamburger, he proceeded to put the frog in his mouth so he could switch hands to eat the burger. I can imagine he would still do that today if he wanted to make someone laugh or just shock them. It would not faze him to stick a frog in his mouth for a good laugh.

His mom also recalled a time when he was only five and participated in a peewee motorcycle race. Blake was wheeling around the course at a pretty good clip when he spotted a turtle slowly rambling across the track. He immediately stopped, got off his little motorcycle, moved the defenseless turtle to the side of the track, and got back on his cycle to finish the race—dead last. While he didn't win a trophy that day, he most assuredly won hearts!

When Dorothy began taking Blake's older sister Endy, a cute little curly-haired blonde, to beauty pageants, she dragged him along. She had heard him singing in his bedroom, recognized some early skills, and entered him in a talent show when he was very young. The only little boy there, he was embarrassed and hesitated to do any more pageants. While Endy loved parading across the stage, making her turns and flashing a smile (all skills that would serve her well later as one of Ada High School's Couganns, a pep/drill team), Blake felt a little uncomfortable with that. He liked the singing part but the modeling, not quite so much. It was his first experience singing in front of an audience and it took a few years to get him to try it again.

I first met Blake when he was about eleven or twelve years old, a typical Oklahoma boy with a mop of hair on top of his head but cut above his ears and neatly trimmed in back. He still had chubby cheeks that any grandma or aunt would be happy to pinch and the same deep dimples when he smiled that he has today.

One day on Blake's bus, years after the fact, we were talking about Ada and talent shows and I told him about entering Monica and Mandy Cash (my nieces) into a contest outside on a flatbed truck at Kmart when they were about five and six years old. We had worked up a pantomime to "Coconut" by Harry Nilsson. I dressed them in hula skirts, coconut bras, and leis. Mandy got to pantomime the part where she cried out in mock pain from the belly ache, "Doooc-tooor." She held her tummy and opened her mouth really wide, giving it her all because it was her only part since her sister did the rest of the song. Mandy was a year younger than Blake and Monica, and small for her age, so she was pretty funny. They didn't win but their performance was obviously memorable to Blake because when I told him about it he unexpectedly said, "I remember that! I was there." We still laugh about that memory from long before he actually knew me or either of them. (Mandy is now a single mom to two children, Denver and Kamryn Davison, and is a successful loan officer for a mortgage company. Monica, who ironically became Blake's first girlfriend, is married to Jeremy Walton, has a son Brody, and is a wonderful teacher and realtor.)

Blake attended Latta Elementary School, one of several schools located in tiny towns surrounding Ada. Shirley and Alton Wood were among his teachers and I later taught with both of them at Konawa Public Schools, which is about twenty miles north of Ada. When Facebook came along, Shirley and I reconnected and she loved to talk about Blake. He had been a pleasure to teach and they remembered him fondly. Alton even showed up in a meet and greet line once and surprised Blake. They were clearly proud of his success.

Dick and Dorothy divorced when Blake was about nine years old. At first he lived with Dorothy and later with Dick. But they still lived relatively close and were always equally supportive of all three of their children. They maintained a friendly relationship with each other as well as the new spouses each later brought into the family.

When Blake transferred from Latta Elementary to Ada Middle School, he met his first girlfriend, my niece Monica, a feisty little blonde who fell for him not because he was a "hunk," but because she thought he was hilarious. They were maybe twelve—puppy love. I'm sure, in an attempt to impress, he recorded a tape for her that covered some of his favorite songs: "Dumas Walker" (written and recorded by The Kentucky Headhunters); "Country Club" (Catesby Jones, Dennis Lord), by Travis Tritt; and "Killin' Time" (Hayden Nicholas, Clint Black), by Clint Black. He had to think he was pretty good to do that sort of thing. And of course, Valentine's Day couldn't go by without the traditional gift every young guy buys for his girl, a stuffed animal. As Monica remembers, Blake's choice was a brown and white bunny rabbit with floppy ears.

I asked Monica what she remembers about those days besides that stuffed bunny rabbit. According to her, one of the things they liked to do was make four-way calls with their favorite couple friends, Jon Parker and Kellye Stafford. Prior to smart phones, kids depended on land lines. The phones were set up for three-way calls, so they would get each other on the line, then Blake would patch in his buddy, and Monica would do the same with hers. Presto, four-way calling! Then the four of them would visit hours on end about all kinds of stuff: school, Tom Petty, Michael Jackson, U2, maybe even TV's *Night Court* or anything else kids that age liked to talk about. Sometimes one of them had to hang up and the others would keep talking. If anyone else was still on the phone and Monica or Blake had to go, Monica would say, "OK Blake, I love you," to which he would reply, "I know you do." It would make her mad that he would only say, "I love you too" if it was just the two of them on the telephone. In more recent years, Blake admitted that Monica was his first kiss.

Those years for Blake were exactly like those years have been for young boys probably since the beginning of time. The breakup between Blake and Monica was typical; it just fizzled out, no great drama. She can't remember if she sent him a note or had a friend tell him, as kids that age do (she didn't mention that he might have broken up with her), but they remained friends. In fact, a few years later, they double-dated to a Christmas dance. Monica's new boyfriend was two years older and had just received his driver's license. It just seemed like the thing to do. (After Blake's success, Monica and her mother-in-law, Joquita Walton, helped with his fan club party a couple of times, enjoying seeing how far he had come.)

When Blake outgrew the beauty pageant days, his mom took him to the Music Palace to audition for *The Country Music Express*. Larry, Gil Ragland, and Jae L. Stilwell had put together a band and produced the Opry-style show, which always included several local performers. The Music Palace was located southeast of the Village Inn, not far out of town. It was the first place live family-friendly entertainment was available in Ada. It was a huge building, but I don't remember how many it actually seated. Upon entry, there was a concession stand operated by my mother, Patricia Keeling. Her specialty was funnel cakes like you could get at state fairs all over. They smelled so good (better than popcorn, even). Patti and her best friend Shelley Ragland, Gil and Barbara's daughter, had planned to work the concession stand, but after one night they figured out they weren't going to get rich overnight and bailed. Monica helped her grandmother sometimes, too. Inside the auditorium itself, the first thing you might have noticed was a huge bubble in the ceiling. Heavy plastic runners were strung across the rafters and undoubtedly there had been a heavy rain, which had left a water bubble hanging behind part of the stretched-out plastic, probably from a leak in the roof. I would never sit anywhere close to that thing. I could just see it bursting and raining down on only me. The back of the stage was painted with a western village scene. When Blake auditioned for a singing spot, his talent and personality shined through and Larry took an immediate liking to him.

Since Blake had sung in the talent portion of a little pageant contest in Pontotoc County, he had some stage experience. They put him in the show. I have a video of his first performance and it reflects a very young guy with a fair degree of self-confidence. Monica remembers Blake being unusually nervous and acting very different from his normal fun-loving self the first time he performed there. He was still a chubby kid in glasses, but once he took the stage, he demonstrated an amazing ability to entertain a crowd. His go-to song of the late 1980s was "Old Time Rock 'n' Roll" (George Jackson), by Bob Seger and the Silver Bullet Band. The crowd loved him! And, it didn't hurt that half the crowd was probably related. His dad had never heard his son sing. Blake told him ahead of time that he would be singing at the Music Palace, so Dick went to the show and sat in the very back of the auditorium. He was surprised by his son's talent and from that moment on was behind him wholeheartedly.

As he delved further into music, much of Blake's inspiration came from his big brother, Richie Shelton, ten years his senior. Technically, he was Blake's half-brother, but no one looked at him in any way other than Dick and Dorothy's son and Endy's and Blake's big brother. Even though Dick was not his biological father, Richie had adopted the name Shelton and always considered Dick his dad. Born in the 1960s, Richie embraced the pop music of the 1970s and 1980s. Blake loved to sit outside Richie's bedroom door and listen to the blaring sounds of ZZ Top and Van Halen coming from that room. (Later, he would add "Sharp Dressed Man" [Billy Gibbons, Dusty Hill, Frank Beard] to the set list on a tour. And one of his fan club parties was dedicated solely to songs from the 1980s. He had several guests and they all enjoyed the retro music of that era.) Music was a big deal to Blake from a very young age. Music, cars, and racing—Dick and Richie loved those things, so

Blake did too. At only twenty-four, Richie was taken far too soon in an automobile accident, along with his fiancé and her young son. Blake was only fourteen and had a difficult time accepting the death of his hero/brother.

I always felt that it helped in dealing with the death of someone special to talk about them, remember the good times. I knew Blake before Richie passed, but I didn't know Richie. I told Blake I would love to know more about him. We made several road trips to and from Nashville and there was a lot of time to talk. The first time I asked, Blake just said that he was a fun guy. He had a difficult time talking about him. Later, as he opened up more, he told me that he had dreams where he would wake up hearing that ambulance siren and be unable to move. At the time the accident happened, Blake and Dick lived in Oakhurst Apartments just off Arlington Street, located very close to Valley View Hospital. He had heard sirens that morning, though he didn't know at the time that they were from Richie's accident. He went to school and Dick had to go get him to give him the sad news a couple of hours later. He was devastated! Fourteen is an impressionable age anyway, and to lose an older brother is just unimaginable.

Blake's very first album was dedicated to Richie. And many more years later, fans in the thousands would come to know him through a song; "Over You" (Blake Shelton, Miranda Lambert) that Dick had encouraged Blake to write. "I'll never get over you" would still be the way Blake felt about Richie more than twenty years later.

Everyone in Blake's family had been encouraging as he grew up. He used to go fishing with his Uncle Dearl Newby, and afterward, his uncle would pull out the guitar and sing a little. Blake was in awe of that ability and took an interest. Newby taught him to play three chords (C, F, and G) on the guitar. (The guitar he learned to play on was featured in the "Ol' Red" video.) Blake used that guitar when he wrote his first song, "That Girl Made a Fool Out of Me," when he was fifteen. He says now it was a piece of crap, but at the time, he thought it was pretty cool.

Even a small biography of each family member who encouraged Blake's success would take up an entire book . . . just so many. But they all played a big part in his career, as did friends he met along the way. Blake had a picture hanging in his first Nashville apartment of his entire family. It literally looked like a town photograph. Blake Shelton has an absolutely unbelievable memory that never ceases to amaze me, and I know he remembers each and every one!

Moving into his high school years, Blake was popular with all the kids. He didn't really hang with any particular clique; he loved everyone and everyone loved him. He did have a few close buddies: Chris "Bird" Childress, Jayson "Buck" Gray (who would later become his merchandise manager for a few years), Cory Coggburn, and Robert Ingram.

Ada was a big football town and the games were a social event for Blake; however, he didn't seem to be the fan he is today. He mainly wandered up and down the sideline visiting with everyone.

Known as a funny guy, he pulled his fair share of pranks. Once he loaded a dead deer that had been hit by a car and left on the roadside into the back of his pickup truck, took it to the school parking lot, and propped it behind the steering wheel of a friend's pickup, giving everyone a story to tell their grandkids in years to come. His buddy Cory was a baseball player while the others participated in football, so in the winter months, Blake and Cory hung out together almost daily. They thought it was fun to take people's yard ornaments, pumpkins, and hay in October, and light-up Santa Clauses in November and December, and relocate them across town to somebody else's yard, even plugging them in. And they never got caught. Blake didn't think relocating was the same as stealing, so had no guilty conscience. He probably thought of himself as a kind of holiday Robin Hood.

Sometime during high school, he tired of messing with glasses and switched to contact lenses. In his first publicity shot (before there was much to publicize), he wore round thin wire-rimmed glasses. At school and around town, he usually dressed in a three-button knit shirt with a collar or a tee shirt under a flannel shirt in cooler months, Wrangler jeans, and tennis shoes. But when he went on stage, Dick made sure his cotton western shirt and jeans were starched and pressed. Dorothy took care of the hairstyle, which remained the same for several years. The mullet was popular in the early 1990s and Blake proudly sported his well past the expiration date. Once Blake liked something, it was difficult to get him to try something new.

His teachers knew he didn't love being inside a classroom and they did all they could to help him keep his grades up to snuff. How could they not enjoy a young man who always had a winning smile and still called adults "Sir" and "Ma'am?" He was known as "just a good ol' country boy," who preferred tennis shoes to cowboy boots. Ashley Loper, assistant editor of *The Cougar Call* (Ada High School paper, 2001) interviewed Blake's former teachers. Richard Truitt's shop class was his favorite class, where he carved tiny wooden guitars and gave them to his friends, and just before graduation, he carved one for Mr. Truitt. On Blake's personality, Truitt said, "He came into class every day wearing a white shirt with a flannel over-shirt and rolled up sleeves, singing [Bing Crosby's version of] 'I'll Be Home for Christmas' [Kim Gannon, Walter Kent, Buck Ram], no matter the time of year. Every day!" *Cougar Call* advisor and journalism teacher Joe Claxton added, "Blake was determined not to do anything in my class. One day I mentioned something about needing an outdoor column. I don't believe he ever looked up from his computer again. He wrote very humorous outdoor columns and stories. He was always complaining about not having enough space in the *Call.*" Loper noted, "His column gave advice on such things as turkey hunting and the proper ways to skin deer. But Blake never passed an opportunity to sing, in talent shows, *Couganns' Spring Show*, just anywhere someone would listen."

The Music Palace had closed but he had started playing at the McSwain Theatre in downtown Ada and was such a crowd pleaser that Paul Alford, the owner, asked him to be a regular. When he found out he would be paid $50 per show, Blake was ecstatic! He would be getting paid for doing what he loved to do. It brings to mind the Mark Twain quote, "Find a job you enjoy doing, and you will never have to work a day in your life."

Alford fixed up the theater a little, but it still had the 1950s style marquee out front that we had grown up with. I made panels for the stage and everyone chipped in to do whatever they could to make it presentable. Townspeople loved it!

That went on for a year or so, and Blake had developed a strong local following. He had asked Larry, band leader and drummer for the show's house band McSwingers, if he would help him move to Nashville. Larry told him that he would do all he could to help him fulfill his dream if he would finish high school first. Blake agreed. When it came time to write his junior term paper, and knowing I taught reading at nearby Konawa, he tried to wheedle me into writing it for him. I told him I couldn't do that but that he could make it work for him. I suggested that he write his paper about the history of country music. He did and I think he made a C on the paper. I was very proud of him and I hope that was one of the things that inspired him to be such an exceptional student of traditional country music. (He knows more about it and more songs of those country greats than anyone I know.)

At sixteen, Blake participated in a statewide contest reminiscent of the old television show *Star Search* called *Oklahoma Kids*. Angie and Mike Stafford have always been huge supporters of Blake. Mike was a local doctor and Angie a nurse. They got Blake involved with *Oklahoma Kids,* and drove him to shows all over the state. The kids would gain points at each show and Blake managed to score enough points in those preliminary rounds to win the top honor, the Denbo Diamond Award, without ever having to compete in the final round. One of 476 acts from across Oklahoma, he won over dancers, Broadway show tune singers, and other theatrical performers with his rendition of "If I Could Bottle This Up" (Paul Overstreet, Dean Dillon). Blake held his own on that stage with his wholesome country twang, and he stood out among all the singers who were belting out their versions of popular songs, no matter how good they were. I think sometimes even things that are great get monotonous. Blake's act was so unique for that show that it was like a breath of fresh air. The win gave Blake's self-esteem a big boost!

The McSwain Theatre remained a big part of Blake's life and ours in those years. Larry and I were both educators and knew how much family loved to see their offspring perform, so we suggested an awards show for the McSwain. There were five categories, and after a set of preliminary shows, semifinals, and finals in each, the event culminated with the awards show. I set up the time frame and suggested that audience members be allowed to vote for their top three favorites and had an outside firm count the votes (I hoped that by choosing three, the cream would rise to the top by each audience member voting for the friend or relative they came to see, plus two real favorites.) The winners would be revealed the night of the awards' presentations. The idea was a cross between a reality talent show and an awards show, with weeks of guaranteed big audiences, which was the real goal. Jae L. Stilwell made a tape of songs to be performed so the band would be ready for rehearsals and she would host and perform at the show. Larry was the bandleader, and Gil Ragland (in addition to running sound) organized the arrival of nominees in classic cars, where they were announced as they walked the red carpet to the front of the theater building. Our daughter Debi Large was responsible for writing the script for the awards' presenters. We made it a big deal. It has stood the test of time and is still an annual event at the McSwain.

Blake wore a suit jacket with jeans and arrived with Robyn and Rachel Brown (local entertainers) to walk the red carpet with a girl on each arm. Regulars were not up for any award, but Blake got to perform in front of the legendary Mae Boren Axton, who cowrote Elvis's "Heartbreak Hotel" (Tommy Durden, Axton, Presley). She also brought along her famous son, Hoyt Axton. He had written many hits but the one that everyone seemed to remember best was "Joy to the World," which had a line about a bullfrog, and he used to always have a pocket full of little bullfrog pins to hand out when he came to town. He was also featured in many movies, including *Gremlins*. The Axton family hails from Oklahoma and Mae had attended college at ECU, so it was a coup to get them both back to Ada. Jae L. had met her years earlier when she and her cousin Debbie Allen were the duo *Queen's Court* and made a trip to Nashville. It didn't hurt that her other son, John, was a local attorney who lived in Ada. Today, you can find Mae's handprints and signature in a cement block in front of the McSwain, just like at Grauman's in Los Angeles.

The highlight of the show was the presentation of the Mae Boren Axton Award for continued support of country music and Oklahoma talent to the award's namesake. Upon accepting the award, Mama Mae said that she was overwhelmed with the level of talent in Ada. Among the performers were Hoyt Axton, Jae L. Stilwell, thirteen-year-old Megan Sheehan, and seventeen-year-old Blake Shelton. When Blake took the stage for one of his songs, he told the audience he had been "sitting backstage visiting with my good friend, Hoyt."

A funny little side note about Hoyt was shared to me by my daughter, Debi. She was sitting in the front row during the performances and happened to be seated right next to Hoyt. At one point, with no warning, Hoyt tapped her on the arm and leaned over and said, "What do you call someone who hangs around musicians?" She told him she didn't know, and Hoyt said, "a drummer." She laughed because her daddy was the drummer in the band on the stage at that moment. Hoyt had the perfect foil.

Little did Blake know that night how Hoyt Axton would also influence his career. Mae loved Blake and encouraged him to relocate to Nashville, another boost to his ego which made him want to move more than ever!

Blake said in his first brief biography, "I'll either earn a living singing country music or picking up cans on the side of the road." There was no Plan B. Blake asked me recently what I thought he would be doing today if he hadn't made it. I told him that there was never any doubt in my mind that he would make it, but he made me answer, so I said, "Construction of some kind." He agreed. But, I maintain that he would have been a weekend warrior as well. He couldn't get too far away from a stage.

The summer before his junior year, Blake had spent those three months working in construction, painting and roofing houses for his stepdad/fishing buddy, Mike Shackleford. Oklahoma summers are brutally hot and humid, and by the time school started in the fall, he had lost all the baby fat and his blue eyes were even more striking without glasses. He had become a tall, thin, handsome young man who had a personality like none I had ever seen in someone so young. He seemed to have an old soul. He was a good listener and he loved to listen to the stories of others. He treated everyone with the same respect. Whether he was talking to a cute girl his age, a four-year-old, or a grandma, he gave each his undivided attention and made each feel special. It is a gift and one that not many possess.

Blake had his *look*, which required his Aunt Betty Newby (Dorothy's sister and Dearl's wife) to alter the legs of his Wranglers assuring a fit just right to suit him. Another Okie, Garth Brooks, had made the Mo Betta collarless and colorful shirt popular and he had a few of those. He wore the shirts tucked into the jeans with a black western belt, and the black cowboy boots that completed his look. On special occasions, he wore a black leather vest with a white shirt. And, a year or so later, I went to Anthony's and got him a looser fitting, jean jacket–style vest to which he took an immediate liking, wearing it until it wore out. He played a shiny black Takamine guitar that he couldn't keep clean enough to suit his dad, who constantly worried about the fingerprints all over it. I carried an extra guitar strap for years just in case he forgot his, and a stick of cosmetic cover for the occasional dreaded teenage zit. Blake Shelton was beginning to get pretty well known around the Ada area, and it was important to him to always look his best onstage. Besides, Dick and Dorothy would have it no other way!

After he had voiced his desire to move to Nashville and get serious about a career in country music, he started to hang around our house quite a bit. If Larry had been encouraged at Blake's age, he would have probably done something similar. He was a drummer and singer and has played music since his high school days. He has been part of well-known area bands in the past and he still plays some in jam sessions around Ada for fun. The money he made when we were in college and through our teaching years came in handy. And one time, he was called in to audition for The Nashville Network's (TNN) *So You Want to be a Star*, but the show went off the air before he could participate. So maybe he did enjoy Blake's enthusiasm vicariously to some degree. Blake was doing what he would have enjoyed doing but didn't get the opportunity. He wanted us to do all we could to help him. Most of our friends thought it was a little crazy that we also moved to Tennessee, but it was the best move we ever made. It definitely made our lives more fulfilling. It is a running gag with me and our daughters on how long it takes Larry to bring up Blake's name when he meets anyone new. He can literally work it into any conversation be it with a waitress, auto mechanic, sales clerk—you name it! Before Dick passed in 2012, he called Larry every day with the same greeting, "How's our boy doing on the charts today?" Those two never tired of talking about Blake. They had so much love and enthusiasm about Blake that people seemed to enjoy hearing them ramble on about him.

We had become friends a few years earlier with the Johnson Sisters (Loudilla, Loretta, and Kay), organizers of IFCO (International Fan Club Organization), so Larry sent them a tape and asked them to allow a couple of the McSwain kids, Blake Shelton and

Megan Sheehan, to perform at their luncheon show that summer. (It wasn't until years later when Loretta Johnson passed and was buried in Elmwood, Oklahoma, that I realized they had a tie to our state.) They agreed and Blake was looking forward to Fan Fair 1994.

During the holiday break, Blake recorded songs (to pre-recorded backing tracks) in Oklahoma City and Tulsa studios in preparation for his first trip to Nashville in March. At the Long Branch Studio, Ed Robinson, a well-known Tulsa musician who had been in the music business for several years, recorded Blake on two songs: Mark Collie's "Shame, Shame, Shame" and Travis Tritt's "Put Some Drive in Your Country." Naively, Larry sent the recordings, which I'm sure were never heard, to some Nashville producers. Still, it was another experience for Blake, and in one of his fan club newsletters, he said at the time, "Recording is a learning experience, and I want to do a lot more of it. Putting together an album would be great. I don't know yet when I will be able to do that, but I hope it is soon. Right now, I am just concentrating on trying to get noticed in Nashville."

We organized a full-fledged concert to raise money for Blake's first Nashville Showcase, and on February 26, 1994, Blake sold out the McSwain Theatre. It might not sound so impressive now, but everyone was super excited on that day! Mike Stafford could not wait to put up the "Sold Out" sign on the marquee. Blake's band included Larry on drums, along with Wayne Morton (steel guitar), Johnnie Bennett (bass guitar), Ronnie Magar (lead guitar), Dale Ozment (harmonica), Lawrence Hinman (piano), and backup singers Hannah Orebaugh and Sheila Brown. Emcee for the evening was Rick O'Brien (brother of Little Texas member Dwayne O'Brien, who was also from Ada) and opening the show were featured vocalists, Megan Sheehan and Jae L. Stilwell. That night, Blake entered the stage into a smoke-filled darkness with a single light on him. He was wearing a long black duster and sang Alan Jackson's "Midnight in Montgomery" (Jackson, Don Sampson).

For Ada, it was first class stuff! We had the entire show videoed and I still watch it from time to time.

He followed that up with a performance at Glenwood Elementary for five-year-old Kasha Perry's *Show and Tell*. The class was studying the letter G and he took his guitar.

Shortly after the success of Blake's concert, promoters of the Little Texas show contacted Larry about the possibility of Blake (along with Tammy Lee, who had recently won *Female Vocalist* at the McSwain Awards show) opening for them when they played Ada, allowing him to play in front of his biggest crowd to date. Blake was happy to sign on the dotted line.

Up and down and up! You have to pray that there are more ups than downs. Every country singer has had to pay dues in some way before hitting it big. Whether he realized it at the time or not, that is what he was beginning to do. I kept a diary of the Nashville trip:

March 11: We left Ada traveling down I-40 to Nashville.

March 12: Blake auditioned for Gaylord Enterprises to perform at Opryland or any of their venues, and sang at the iconic Libby's Steakhouse and live radio show (which was destroyed by fire in 2013) in Elkton, Kentucky.

March 13: Sunday was spent touring the Opryland Hotel gift shops and performing at the Nashville Palace.

March 14: We spent the day calling people about the showcase. Blake visited with former Conway Twitty guitarist Charlie Archer (Oklahoma friend), and made the final preparations for his showcase on Tuesday. We also attended the *Music City Tonight* television show as guests of Mae Axton. Blake got to meet Charlie Chase, Shelby Lynn, Clinton Gregory, and Shawn Camp. Blake took a portfolio to the show's talent coordinator for a possible booking on the show. Blake rehearsed for tomorrow's showcase.

March 15: Blake performed his showcase and received great response. He met Loudilla, Loretta, and Kay, the Johnson Sisters from IFCO. (Just before the trip, Ada mayor Ray Stout had proclaimed March 15, 1994, as Blake Shelton Day in Ada, because they wanted to show their "confidence in his success *before* he actually became successful.")

March 16: Blake met with Clay Myers of Starstruck, Reba McEntire's company, and performed at the Bull Pen Lounge.

March 17: Blake visited with Chip Hardy and Stroudavarious Publishing.

The showcase for Megan Sheehan (6:30 p.m.) and Blake Shelton (7:00 p.m.) took place on Tuesday March 15, 1994, at SIR on Fifth Avenue South in Nashville, Tennessee. We chose an early time thinking we could catch industry people on their way home from work. We offered food and drink in an effort to get them there. We had absolutely no idea what we were doing! There was a crowd, though, and it was a great experience for Blake.

After the show, there was a lot of beer and soda left and so as not to waste it, Larry ran to a nearby convenience store and picked up a Styrofoam ice chest and a bag of ice. We loaded it up with the leftovers and headed back to the motel. As Larry was unlocking the door to the room, we could hear the phone ringing. Thinking someone important might be calling (ha ha), Larry raced into the room, dropping the ice chest and cracking it open, sending beer, pop, and ice scattering all over the floor from the cheap container. At the same time, he proceeded to sail across a bed and grab the phone on the second or third ring. Blake was laughing so hard he could barely breathe! I'm telling you, that move should be incorporated somewhere in the Olympics. It was a sight to behold.

Nothing big happened that week. Blake didn't get a job at Opryland as we had hoped, and that may have been an unanswered prayer. Nobody was rushing to sign him up, but he did gain some experience meeting people and performing and was getting anxious to move there to jumpstart his career. Megan, another McSwain protégé, and her mother were along on most of the activities mentioned above. Megan was just entering high school and was not ready for the move yet, but she is so talented. She and Blake used to do some duets together and I loved that. She would later attend college at Belmont and receive a degree in music business. When we were all running around Opryland Hotel, Blake tried to sneak Megan some ice cream. Gayle Sheehan (her mom) didn't think it was good for her voice and she would be singing that week at the IFCO luncheon too. We had met Clay Myers earlier when we (Larry, Gil Ragland, and I) had taken Jae L. Stilwell to Nashville in 1990 and he recorded her with backing tracks. Clay worked for Reba and he was a very nice guy! And, many years later, Megan would get a deal with James Stroud at *Stroudavarious Records* just before it folded, never getting to release her music. That just gives you an idea of how fluid this business can be. There wasn't a Warner Bros. to pick up her contract and despite her talent, she hasn't been able to get another label deal.

Blake also performed at the State Fair of Oklahoma, AdaFest, and at several benefit concerts throughout the state. It was a big year for him. Before he even sang one note at the State Fair performance, he was besieged for autographs. One group of young ladies asked him to sign dollar bills because they believed he would be bigger than Garth Brooks.

Music was beginning to consume a lot of his time, but Blake was still in high school and was not going to get to make the big move until he walked across that stage and got his diploma. Larry insisted that was necessary to becoming a role model.

Blake was starting to write songs and would sing for anyone who would listen. Dorothy was running a karaoke night at the Village Inn, a club in Ada, and he developed a love for that too. He didn't talk much about school but he did enjoy his friends and they had started coming to his shows. Larry was preparing for the move, as promised, and there were a few trips to Nashville that last semester of his senior year.

Upon deciding Blake needed a manager to help further his career, Larry enlisted Mae Axton to help him find one that would work for commission only. Larry has always loved air travel, and used it as an excuse to book their flight to Nashville. I snapped a photograph in the lobby of Will Rogers World Airport in Oklahoma City, and Blake looks so very young. He has the mullet and is wearing a multicolored large-checked knit shirt with a solid color band around the collar and sleeves, faded jeans tucked in without a belt, and dark high-top tennis shoes. His eyes are puffy underneath and I bet he had been so excited that he hadn't slept the night before. There was still just a little chubbiness in his cheeks at age seventeen.

Steve Cropper (great guitarist, songwriter, and producer) had a big office in the same building as Blake's potential manager, who had a tiny office upstairs in the back. When we met with Jim Sharp, he used Cropper's office which was far more impressive. It was also necessary as his little office wouldn't have held four people unless they were standing shoulder to shoulder like sardines in a can. Blake didn't have much to say that day. Larry and Sharp did most of the talking. After the meeting, we spent the remaining time there going around to local hangouts like Buddy Killen's Stockyard Bull Pen Lounge and the Nashville Palace, where Randy Travis had worked as a cook. Mae went there with us and I remember her shushing us during one of the performances. We thought that was just the Bluebird that demanded silence. Everyone else was talking. But *we* didn't talk anymore!

Sharp immediately gave Blake a personal management agreement. After hearing nightmare stories of managers, Larry suggested Blake take the contract to local Ada attorney John Axton (Mae's son) to read, and he returned it to Blake on June 23, 1994, with suggestions for edits. After almost a year, Blake did sign on March 24, 1995, with Larry as the witness.

On October 22, 1994, Blake had the pleasure of performing a concert during a day of tributes to local rodeo/talent businessman Ken Lance. It kicked off with a parade, and Blake was there riding a horse, something you don't see often. Country music stars Alan Jackson, Brooks & Dunn, Chris LeDoux, Mel Tillis, Marty Stuart, and many more sent their well wishes and items to be used in an auction during the fun. Blake's fan club managed to get a pair of tennis shoes autographed by Willie Nelson to donate. A booklet was printed, giving details of Ken's long and illustrious career, and as a performer at the tribute, Blake had a double page, picture and biography. I asked him to autograph my copy that day and to write something original. He did just that: "Carol, Something Original. Blake." Larry put together a special band, which included Charlie Archer, Ronnie Magar, Wayne Morton, Tony Nickell, Furmon Huff, and Larry.

Always a favorite, later that month Blake was voted "Favorite Local Entertainer" by readers of the *Ada Evening News*, an honor he would hold for a few years, until it became obvious that he was no longer just a local entertainer.

And not much later, Blake had the pleasure of actually reopening the Ken Lance Sports Arena, located thirteen miles southeast of Ada near Stonewall, Oklahoma, to a capacity crowd. (Larry was the drummer for the Country Lancers, who had been the house band there for more than a decade, which included the year Blake was born.) Known for its big rodeos, the dance hall had become an area favorite as well. The rodeo came first and then one year, Ken and Ruth had set up a jukebox on a slab of concrete so people could dance after the rodeo. They loved it!

Being a first class entrepreneur, Ken decided to build a metal building around it and a huge stage big enough for two bands so there would be no down time between the opening act and the main one. Through the years, the entry to the dance hall had become completely filled floor to ceiling with autographed pictures of all the stars that had appeared there. During the rodeo, stars were pulled out into the arena on a flatbed trailer for a performance and later in the evening, played at the dance hall. Every major singer from that era made an appearance: Loretta Lynn, Willie Nelson, George Jones, Jack Greene, Mel Tillis, and many, many others. Reba McEntire, who grew up in nearby Chockie, got her start there. Blake's hope was that playing at Ken Lance's would be as lucky for him as it was for Reba.

Reopening this great old dance hall was an experience Blake wouldn't forget. It was also one of the first full-fledged dances he had headlined. The place smelled of the popcorn that kept patrons thirsty and going back for more beer. By now, it had a great wooden dance floor and tables all around it three or four deep. Ken was a showman. He could do rope tricks and often did to get people wound up before the band started playing. He wore a giant foam cowboy hat and threw an illuminated lasso around and around. Everyone loved Ken, Stonewall's own rhinestone cowboy. Blake loved the venue. Growing up, everyone that loved country music went there on Saturday night. There were a whole flock of Byrds (Dorothy's family) who were familiar faces there and Blake had heard all their stories. It was a goal to actually perform at a dance there. And, he joked, "see a fight."

The next two months were a blur as Blake was wrapping up his high school days with end-of-the-year activities, getting ready to graduate and *move*!

CHAPTER TWO

IT AIN'T EASY

Blake did it! He graduated high school at the big gold Kerr Dome at ECU on May 19, 1994, and two weeks later he was ready to move to Music City. We loaded him up and drove there in our white Chevrolet Suburban. I usually let him sit in front because, though it was a big vehicle, it was not big enough for Blake's long legs. Even with the front passenger seat pushed as far back as it could go, he managed to knock loose the plastic pipes that carried the air conditioning under the dash. Nothing ever quit working, but that stuff hung loose for the duration of the vehicle's life.

On that move to Nashville, we stopped for a late lunch at Spaghetti Warehouse in Memphis. Blake, at the tender age of seventeen, had a couple of expressions that Larry discouraged. One was when he was in disbelief about something, he would exclaim, "Christ on the cross!" During our lunch that day, he responded to something one of us had said with that phrase, and Larry again reprimanded him that if he was famous and said that, it would make tabloid headlines blaring "Blake Shelton Slams Jesus Christ!" Blake got a big kick out of that but it was true enough. Sometimes, without thinking, we carelessly say things that might be offensive to others but it isn't too big a deal. Celebrities must be more diligent about everything they say because something taken out of context can be exploited and possibly ruin a career. Headlines are meant to grab attention but too many people never read past the headlines.

We got to Nashville and checked into a motel. There was a loft bedroom for Larry and I and a bed downstairs under the loft for Blake. There was also a little kitchen and living area downstairs in the front. One evening, we were just sitting around, Blake and I in the living area with him picking on his guitar while Larry was popping corn right across from us. Only Larry could get bored waiting for microwave popcorn, so he opened the door to a big cabinet that housed the hot water tank and spotted a very large manila envelope propped up on its side. He pulled it out, placed it on the bar between us, and started looking.

Shortly he yelled, "These are Willie Nelson's x-rays!" We didn't take him seriously but he kept pulling x-rays from the envelope and going on and on about them, so finally Blake broke down and got up to see. Blake was shocked to see that there were indeed several x-rays, all with Willie's name on them. On the outside of the envelope were signatures of people, nurses and doctors we presumed, who had checked them out. Larry figured someone stole them and then got scared and just left them there. Blake thought they were probably checked out by Willie and he or one of his crew put them there, only to forget them. We couldn't agree on how they must have ended up in a hot water closet. All I could think was, "What a great story for Blake to tell when he gets on the *Tonight Show* someday." (See, I never doubted he would go places, big places. I used to tell him when he got to be on *Saturday Night Live*, he had to take me, and a few years ago, he did just that! He was the host *and* musical guest—my proud moment! I had watched that show from the beginning, actually at about the time Blake was conceived.) But, back to those x-rays! Larry wanted to get them back to Willie so he called Mae Axton and she said she could do that. We turned them over to her and I assume Willie got his x-rays back.

It is no wonder Blake enjoyed hearing Larry's stories. I've heard them all a million times and I still get a kick out of them because something new is always added. He has a lot of them and many involve former country stars. Now, Larry and his curious nature had found Willie Nelson's x-rays and a new story to add to his growing collection. We couldn't believe it, but we witnessed it. Had he been alone, we would never have believed him. Larry is renowned as someone who can take a story that is great (or not) and embellish it with such flourish at each narration that it becomes legend.

Blake couldn't quit laughing because it was such a Larry thing. He was always brushing up against greatness. He had convinced Conway Twitty and his band to play against his football booster club for a benefit game when he was a coach at Noble, Oklahoma, in the 1970s. Who does that? Conway was huge at that time and after the game, he did a mini concert. Twitty sang his current hit, "I Can Tell You've Never Been This Far Before" and left me thinking, "It isn't a great song choice for an audience of mostly junior high kids and their parents." As far as I know, nobody complained.

And once after spending the night in Ada following a dance at Ken Lance's, we took Lefty Frizzell home with us to feed him a homemade hamburger before taking him to the airport. He asked for a glass so he could have a shot of whiskey, which he carried in his briefcase, and the only small glass I had was a little Flintstone jelly glass. It is a funny memory of that legendary country singer. I also remember he had his wife's name, ALICE, tattooed on his left hand, a letter on each finger. He was very nice and left us an autographed demo record of "You Babe" (Sanger D. Shafer) that I still have. Patti was just a little girl and she liked him because she thought his name was Electric Frizzle (like sizzle). Debi was at that age where she wasn't impressed by much of anything. After the burger, I took a couple of pictures and Larry drove him from our home in Noble to nearby Oklahoma City where he claims they ran through Will Rogers World Airport with Lefty actually singing his big hit, "Always Late" (Frizzell, Blackie Crawford). Embellishment? You tell me.

I can't talk about Larry's brushes with greatness and not mention the great Reba McEntire. Larry asked her to write the liner note on an album the Country Lancers (Larry, Furmon Huff, Dusty Rhodes, Sid Manuel, Tom Trivitt, and Jim Napier) had recorded. They had backed the Singing McEntires (Reba, Pake, and Susie) at the Ken Lance Sports Arena when Reba was still in her teens.

Blake had heard all of those stories more than once and probably again on the drive to Nashville. But our goal was a little different that time. We weren't there for a showcase or running around to places that would allow him to get up and sing or even to meet a potential manager. This time Blake was actually moving to Nashville, fulfilling a dream he had nursed for a while.

We started looking at apartments for him to rent and some were pretty bad. Still, it was kind of fun driving around looking at places. Even though he always managed to have at least a part-time job and everyone chipped in with money when they could, he was on a budget. That wasn't a problem for Blake because he has never been a reckless spender or materialistic person. (You may laugh when you read this today because he does have several residences, a jet, helicopter, and tons of lake toys, but if it all disappeared, he would be fine with it. Necessities would be a guitar, a fishing pole, a rifle, and a shotgun. Those things make him happy anywhere.)

Blake's move had been on Dick's and Dorothy's minds since he had voiced his desire to go through with it. I remember there was a country artist just getting started about a year earlier, while Blake was still merely talking about his move. He had been making the rounds on The Nashville Network on shows like Ralph Emery's *Nashville Now*, telling stories about sleeping in alleys and that sort of thing. Dorothy threatened Blake with his life if he ever played the "poor me" card. While he didn't grow up a child of wealth, he had always had a good home. Once, after looking at a particularly sleazy apartment, Blake actually lamented, "Please don't make me live here." He said it in a silly voice but he really did mean it. I know he wanted to move but it had to be a little scary, and I know he was concerned about driving in a big city.

We kept looking until we found an appropriate place for him to live, 704 Berry Road, close enough to downtown Nashville, actually pretty close to Douglas Corner, which is where he had his first real showcase and his first Nashville fan club party. His rent was about $300 per month, and there was a policeman living next door, so we thought it was perfect. We planned to stay with him until he turned eighteen and then return home, leaving him in the big city alone except for knowing only a couple of people, namely Mae Axton and his manager.

Just hanging out in his manager's office allowed Blake the opportunity to meet people who quickly took a liking to the admirable young man who had made a life-changing move at the age of seventeen. Absolutely no one was with him that first six months before his big sister, Endy, graduated college and moved there too, but he never had trouble making friends.

Dorothy had given me an envelope full of money for Blake, but we wanted to leave that in the bank for him. We shopped for furniture in used furniture stores and got him set up. I insisted he have a new mattress but it was a lousy one because it was so cheap. We weren't exactly loaded either, but where a mattress was concerned, I thought cleanliness was more important than comfort. Still, it was probably a good thing he was so young and his bones could handle anything. We got him a bed frame and a used sleeper sofa, which is where we slept while we were there. The springs in the sofa were so bad that we pulled the mattress onto the floor and slept there in the living area. I sprayed it with Lysol disinfectant to be on the safe side. Somebody in the family (Endy I think) gave him a small blue table and chairs. He barely had enough furniture to call it a residence, but that didn't matter because he was in Nashville for one reason and one reason only: to get a label deal and record songs!

Meanwhile, that same week, Blake was set to perform at the June 8 IFCO Luncheon Show during Nashville's Fan Fair '94, which came with the opportunity to sign autographs in their booth. We had printed photos for him to give away, and he sat at a bar, along with a long line of newcomers sprinkled with an occasional well-known act, signing pictures and having his own photo taken by country music enthusiasts. Savvy fans had learned that they could get pictures with newcomers and that some of them would later become famous. I believe they saw some potential in his look and personality even before they heard him sing.

While he was signing, we sat in some folding chairs against a wall outside of and to the side of the booth enjoying watching him interact with people. At some point, I went to the restroom and met a group of girls wearing "I Hate Garth" buttons. I told them I was from Oklahoma and that we were pretty proud of Garth Brooks there, and even if they didn't like him, wasn't there someone they could support rather than be negative about him? They just looked at me and walked away. The weird thing about some people and celebrity is that they build them up until they have them on a high pedestal and then seem to enjoy knocking them off of it. I didn't get it then and I don't get it now. I told Blake about the encounter and he couldn't believe it either.

It was an exciting time. The event's twenty-four thousand tickets that year had sold out in February. Old timers remember Fan Fair fondly. It was held at the old fairgrounds and was the precursor to what is now the CMA Music Festival. June was usually hot and humid and there was a state fair atmosphere to the event, making it seem perfectly normal for young women to run back and forth between the exhibit halls and the concerts in bathing suit tops. The stage for shows was in a lower area and the trek up and down that hill to and from the stage got more difficult as the temperature rose. How hot was it? Daughter Patti claimed she was hotter than the proverbial $3 bill. Once, as we were all going back up the hill following a concert, she jokingly (I think) offered one smiling man in a golf cart $100 to drive her up the hill. He just smiled and kept driving.

After the Fan Fair experience, the first thing Blake did was call Mae Axton, who had encouraged the move, and asked what she wanted him to do next. He probably thought she would have some singing gigs in mind. But she said, "Well, you can come paint my gazebo." She was getting her place ready for a big family reunion. Blake always says he painted her house because that sounds better, but it *was* only a gazebo and a few other added odd jobs.

Sometime during the job, she gave him a tiny old black and white television and he was good to go, happy to have something to watch when he was home alone. (Maybe it was Endy who later brought a normal size color television into the apartment, and Mae's set made its new home in a closet. I don't think he ever gave it back to her.)

He again met and became better acquainted with Hoyt Axton during that time. Hoyt was visiting his mother but staying on his bus in her driveway. Both being strong-willed, they butted heads occasionally, and he probably thought there could be too much togetherness. Hoyt had seen Blake sitting down outside during a break and invited him onto his bus. He showed him a knife and shared the interesting history that went with it. Not as impressed with the knife as he was a song that would become his signature, "Ol' Red," Blake remembers Hoyt's booming voice and how he kept beat with his hand on the table as he sang. He made the decision right there that when he got to do an album, that song would go on it.

After he had started working for her, painting and doing odd jobs, Mae invited us all out to her home on the day Blake turned eighteen to surprise him with some take-out chicken and a birthday cake. It was a beautiful old house, so old that her floors squeaked as you walked across them. Hoyt was there too but he stayed on his bus. Mae was annoyed at her son and pressured Blake to go out there and make him come inside to have lunch with the rest of us. But Hoyt was not going to come inside to eat chicken and cake; however, he did give Blake the knife for his birthday, making him wish he had listened to the earlier story more closely. Eventually she begrudgingly sent some lunch out to Hoyt on the bus.

Mae gave Blake a small autographed book of poetry she had written called *From the Window of My Heart (Poems to Live By)*, which was illustrated by her son Hoyt. She inscribed it "Best of the best Blake, I really believe you're close to that big door to a great future in the music business. Stay the fine young man you are now always! Love and God Bless! Mae Boren Axton (Hope you enjoy my thoughts in this little book)."

I tried to get him to read it, telling him he should read at least one poem in case she ever asked him if he had read it. The thing about Blake is that he has always been an excellent listener but not big on reading. His response was, "You read it to me." We were in the car headed somewhere and I was in the back seat. I read a couple of poems aloud, we discussed them a little, and I still have the book. I remember one being about Elvis.

After Blake turned eighteen, he was able to set up his own bank account, so he took the envelope of money Dorothy had sent and headed to the bank. Later, we had a little lesson on how to keep a checkbook and hang on to receipts. I actually did his income tax returns for a couple of years back then, which wasn't difficult. I wish I'd kept copies just for posterity. He was set up in an apartment and had his pickup truck. I tried to make his apartment look homey. I bought a plant for the front room, but he never watered it even once, and left that pitiful little dead plant hanging there until he moved. I also got him a bedside lamp with a cute shade printed with fish and fishing lures. It was gone the next time we visited, replaced by a floor lamp with an LED light that would actually light the room. I never said anything about it because I realized that he thought my choice was entirely too girly. He had accent pieces like a hook made from a turkey foot with the toes placed so that the middle toe was up, making it appear the foot was actually flipping you off. He had a couple of small stuffed animals (not the fluffy kind you buy at Hallmark), skins, and deer heads scattered around. It was 100 percent *Design by Blake*.

Basically, he was set up to live in Nashville. He knew a couple of people and was ready to start working toward a career. When it came time for us to go home, Blake really didn't want us to go. He didn't think he could drive well in Nashville and he didn't know anybody his own age. He couldn't get in clubs without a parent until he was twenty-one. (Larry would say we were his parents, and security must have thought we adopted him as we are much shorter.) He knew we didn't have to go, us being educators and it being summertime, but we talked it over and decided the longer we waited, the more difficult it would be for him. I can still see him in my mind's eye, sitting in the little entry at the front of his apartment with his guitar as we drove away.

He had no idea it was hard for us too. (It reminded us of moving Debi right out of college for her first job in Temple, Texas, five hours away from us.) It would be another six months before Endy graduated college and moved out there with him. During that time, Blake became a loyal viewer of the *Jerry Springer Show*. He loved the outlandishness of that show and he got me watching it a little bit. I remember on one show, a woman took her wooden leg and hit her boyfriend or husband with it. That was my favorite episode. Blake enjoyed all of them. And, he spent a lot of time on the phone. I know I talked with him an hour or so almost every night and I'm sure Dorothy and Dick did the same. He also talked to Patti a lot, and one of those calls would come back to haunt him. And, we did visit often. He got much better on the guitar during that time too! Everything happens for a reason!

Everyone knew Blake would be lonesome and lost, but he was doing what he had decided he needed to do and it was a good decision. One of Blake's old girlfriends sent him some Ada dirt after he moved so he wouldn't forget his roots. I know she thought it was sweet (I did), but he thought it was silly, proving John Gray's book *Men Are from Mars, Women Are from Venus* is a must read for everyone. Don't get the idea he had a bunch of girlfriends either. In Ada, the high school quarterback was the guy every girl wanted to date. I guess because Blake had a baby face, his earliest fans were older and I kept wondering when the younger girls were going to see that he was a catch.

He plugged along with not a lot to do the first few months. His aunts Maryida Ward and Betty Newby sent him care packages of food and his parents sent him money every month. We sent him what we could as well. It bothered him to take the money, but I told him that he should give it at least four years before he became concerned. Endy had chosen to go to college while he had chosen a different path, and neither was free. He made a little money on his own almost from the beginning, doing odd jobs around town. Even then, he said, "I want to make enough money someday that Mom doesn't have to stand all day in a beauty salon." He has always had a big heart and a soft spot for his mama.

One story he told us was about pulling up to an ATM to get some money one night, and he saw Tanya Tucker leaning out of her car. It caught him off guard and he pointed at her yelling, "*Tanya Tucker!*" like she didn't know who she was. She laughed and said something like "Hello cowboy," and drove away waving, leaving him feeling stupid. We were the same way when we moved there. Celebrities were everywhere but most people never bothered them. I saw Donna Summer one day in Trees and Trends, Tanya in Target, Carl Smith in the checkout line at K-Mart. I could go on and on; it was just an everyday thing once you got used to it.

Conscious of the fact that he had pretty much nailed down his look by the time he moved, I suppose we started focusing on his actual physical self. He had a gap in his teeth on the upper right side that was only noticeable when he smiled big. You can see the gap in early photos. I liked his big smile though and thought he should have the gap fixed and Larry agreed. We talked with his parents about it and Dick quickly agreed although Dorothy wasn't so sure; she liked it because it was *Blake* and she liked him just the way he was. I don't remember him even caring one way or the other, leaving it to the adults and he hadn't realized yet that he was one. In the end, Dorothy lost the argument and Dick had the tooth fixed for him. Nobody can disagree that he has one of the nicest smiles in Nashville or anywhere else for that matter.

The year 1994 was much bigger than any of us realized at the time. In the first six months alone, Blake had his first sold-out concert, his first showcase, his first move to another state, his first apartment, and his first Fan Fair, and all those things happened when he was still seventeen years old. By the time he turned eighteen, he was on his own and working toward what he hoped would be his lifetime occupation as a singer/songwriter.

Blake seemed to have an instinct for doing the right thing at the right time, even though sometimes things moved slower than he would have liked. I know he owes a lot of that to his dad. Dick was an honorable man and he was constantly giving Blake advice that he thought went in one ear and out the other, but a lot of it stuck. He even wrote Blake a lengthy letter shortly after his move to Nashville, giving him some advice on how to live his life. Blake doesn't remember even reading the letter all the way through at the time, but he did save it and many years later, after his dad passed, he finally read it. He just doesn't like to read that much; not sure he will even read a book about himself. (Blake, text me "hello" if you've read this far.)

By the time 1995 rolled around, Blake's sister Endy had graduated college mid-year and made the move to Nashville, quickly landing a job at a major computer firm, and she and Blake were soon able to move to a bigger apartment in nearby Brentwood (located between Nashville and Franklin). Everyone was a little more comfortable knowing that he had somebody from home there with him.

Blake got a job at Anne Murray's publishing company, Balmur Music, screening new material. He loved hanging out with those songwriters, but it didn't last long because he soon signed a publishing contract with Naomi Martin Music, which allowed him to devote all of his time to songwriting and his career. And rumor has it that he was fired at Balmur for visiting with songwriters more than doing his job. He never told us that. His new schedule was more flexible and he did a little sign painting on the side for a while; I have a fading memory of him proudly showing us one of those signs sitting up high on steel posts like a billboard.

Soon he cut a new demo tape at Ground Star Laboratories with songs he had collaborated on with Naomi Martin and her daughter, Dale Daniel, who was a recording artist in the early 1990s. Naomi had penned songs recorded by such artists as Ronnie Milsap and Charlie Pride. She had a Grammy nomination for Milsap's "Let's Take the Long Way Around the World" (Archie Jordan, Naomi Martin). With credentials like that, Blake was excited to be working with true industry professionals and beginning his recording career. His plan was to shop the tape to record companies and hope that later in the year he would be given the opportunity to record his own album and begin performing live full time.

He also met with David Preston at Broadcast Music, Inc. (BMI) and signed an agreement where they would audit all performances of songs written by him, ensuring he would get paid for use of his work. BMI is the largest of the three organizations that track songs played on radio, television, and at live shows, making sure that the songwriter gets his fair share of the profits. His first check was just over two dollars and must have been from Ada radio stations KADA and KYKC playing his music.

Blake returned to Fan Fair again and was surprised that a couple of fans, known only as Tina from Florida and Gloria from Illinois, brought photos they had taken the prior year to get signed. His fan base was beginning to grow. His manager owned a magazine (*American Songwriter*) and he was able to sign autographs in that booth. His family came that year and it was fun to watch the crowd around Blake even though he didn't even have a production deal at the time. Once, the line for his autograph wrapped around the corner as Dick, Dorothy, Endy, and Larry stood back against a wall and watched in amazement. I stayed in the booth with him to help with pictures but was just as fascinated as they were by the attention Blake was getting. We were all so proud of him!

While he didn't get to record his own album just yet, he did begin travelling some. Larry was doing his bookings and we still lived in Oklahoma, so that is where he was getting to play. His first road job with his own band was SapulpaFest in Sapulpa, Oklahoma. Debi was editor of the *Sapulpa Daily Herald* and chairman of the SapulpaFest entertainment committee at the time and got him the job. I still have the contract where he was paid $1,300 for a three-hour outdoor concert on August 19, 1995. Just before Blake took the stage was the introduction of Miss Oklahoma 1995, Shawntel Smith, who went on to become Miss America 1996. A simple stage on a flatbed truck was witness to a couple of Oklahoma winners that Saturday night!

The following week, he played the State Shriners' Convention in Oklahoma City. Then a couple of weeks after that, he returned to Ada's Agri-Plex to open for Little Texas for just $1,000. In the list of expenses, it showed paying the five band members $125 each, and beside that a note that Blake wanted to make it $150. He still paid the manager $100, but Larry didn't charge for booking. Bob Rose, from Ardmore, Oklahoma, provided a bus for a mere $150, probably barely covering his expenses. (The bus didn't bring the band from Nashville, just picked them up at our house on Kirby and took them to and from the venue.) Despite that, by my math, Blake made zero unless Larry paid for the bus, which I'd bet he did. Even if that was the case, Blake only made $150. It was noted in the contract that his band wouldn't play for other artists and that Blake would be the last act before Little Texas. Blake just wanted to play and Larry wanted to make Blake look like the star he would become. Priorities!

Oklahoma had made the news in a big way a few months earlier on April 19, 1995, with the bombing of the Alfred P. Murrah Federal Building in Oklahoma City. Domestic terrorists used a moving van equipped with a bomb that destroyed a third of the building, killing 168 people and injuring almost seven hundred others. Fifteen children who were in the America's Kids Day Care Center located in the building were among the dead. Buildings and cars for blocks around were damaged as well. It remains the biggest homegrown terrorist attack in our nation's history.

Shortly after that, on one of his trips back to Oklahoma, Larry and I asked Blake to go up there with us to see the damage first-hand. We were all shocked by the extent of the devastation. We didn't get in the way; the initial rescue work had been done but there remained much to do. Windows were broken out for blocks surrounding ground zero. It was a sad moment in Oklahoma's history, but we wanted to witness what had happened firsthand and felt that Blake would later be glad that he had too. There isn't much to say about that day as all three of us were unusually quiet on the drive back to Ada.

When he got back home, Blake performed for a group of young adults at the Wilson County Youth Emergency Shelter in Lebanon, Tennessee, and returned a few more times to Oklahoma for dances at the Ada Rodeo, Country Rose (which was formerly known as The Coachlight), Buffalo's (which was formerly Ken Lance Sports Arena), and a kick-off campaign dinner for Governor Bill Anoatubby of the Chickasaw Nation. Larry was still playing drums, serving as road manager, and booking most of Blake's shows. We had an apartment behind our house that we had fixed up for daughter Patti and David Binger to live in temporarily and they had moved out, so it was available for his band to use when they played locally. I tried to keep them fed but I have never liked to cook. I remember my mother bringing them soup one day and they thought they had died and gone to heaven, it was so good.

Blake usually stayed with Dorothy when they did shows in Oklahoma. On one of those trips back, he had a card waiting for him at his mom's house. Earlier, on a call to Patti, they had played a game of "tell me something about yourself nobody else knows" and he made the mistake of telling her about an early girlfriend. He had met an older woman and didn't learn until later that she was married. Patti lived in Ada at the time and coincidentally, right after Blake told her the story, she found the woman's picture in a newspaper advertisement for the business where she worked. The wheels started turning and Patti quickly cut the picture out of the paper and headed to her brother-in-law's house to peruse his collection of old 1950s *Playboy* magazines until she found a black and white nude that was the correct size for her anticipated project. She created a one-of-a-kind card, putting the woman's head on the pin-up's body, cutting out the arms and attaching them back with little accordion-style folded papers so that when the card was opened, the arms popped out pointing at him. The sentiment on the card was the title of a song that was being played on the radio at the time ad nauseam, Tim McGraw's big hit, "I Like It, I Love It, I Want Some More of It" (Jeb Stuart Anderson, Steve Dukes, Mark Hall). She had it ready for the next time he would be coming to Ada and mailed it so it would be there when he arrived. I wish I had seen that card! When Blake opened it, he let out his infamous one loud note, *"Ha!"* (Dorothy's laugh) so thunderous in fact that his mother came to see what happened. I don't think he ever told her. If he hasn't, she knows now. Blake and Patti have never changed, still ornery as ever!

Blake had dated a couple of girls in high school before he had his first serious relationship. Ashley Stephenson was a long-distance girlfriend after he moved, even making a trip with us to see him before she graduated. She moved to Knoxville, Tennessee, for college after she finished high school a year later. He did things like make popcorn balls (I remember because he called me for a recipe) to take when he went to see her. And, she did something no other girl has done before or since. She convinced him to wear a pair of khaki shorts and polo shirt to a sorority event once. I would love to have a picture of that! She was a sweet girl; I just don't think they had a lot in common other than having attended Ada High School together and all that encompassed. Even though they were both in Tennessee, it was a three-hour drive from Nash-ville to Knoxville so they didn't see each other often. If memory serves correct, they broke up about midway through her freshman year of college. I still follow Ashley on Facebook and she now has a lovely family.

That fall, Megan Sheehan made the semifinals of the *Jimmy Dean Country Showdown* held at the Wildhorse Saloon in Nashville, and had brought a lot of people from Oklahoma with her to the show. We scheduled a visit for that time so we could see her performance and visit Blake and Endy. Anyone under twenty-one was required to have a parent or guardian. Blake could have easily gone in with us, but nooooo; he wanted to use a fake identity card that he had managed to obtain. It must have been a pretty lousy one because they caught it at the door immediately, cut it in half, told him that he was lucky they didn't call the police, and sent him on his way. At that point, they wouldn't let him in even with our authorization; I am sure they wanted to teach him a lesson. Larry wouldn't leave him outside by himself, so they walked up and down Broadway until the show was over. Endy and I weren't going to miss out on Megan's performance so we stayed for the show. To this day, Blake swears that he has no memory of that event, but I remember it vividly! I really think he does too—just doesn't want to admit it. He has a memory like an elephant.

In March 1996, Blake went home once again for his very first Fan Club Party at the old Aldridge Hotel in downtown Ada, just a block off Main Street. More than two hundred fans and friends joined together to hear Blake perform an unplugged set. His mother recorded the performance and a highlight was his rendition of Paul Overstreet's "I'm Seein' My Father in Me" (Overstreet, Taylor Dunn), dedicated to his own dad. His grandmother didn't live to see his rise to fame but she was at that event, making it an especially important memory for Blake. His stepfather Mike Shackleford built the stage, sister Endy designed invitations, family and friends brought food, the fan club provided soft drinks, and friend Jerry Collier did sound. I think it shows the love and support shown Blake early in his career and it was capped off by the fact that his own mother helped mop up the mess after the party. The fan club signed up twenty-four new members!

Back in Nashville, *The Young Riders* was organized to showcase the talent of young singer/songwriters: Blake Shelton, Amber

Leigh, Rachel Proctor, Kenny Horton, Ryan Murphey, Pete (Mroz) Mitchell (who would show up many years later as a contestant on *The Voice*), and Robin English. Brenda Cline (Artists Concepts), Jim Sharp (*American Songwriter* magazine), and Mervyn Louque (Douglas Corner Café) sponsored the group. They performed the first Tuesday of each month at the Douglas Corner Café. They also got to perform at the famed Bluebird Café, and country network TNN (The Nashville Network) featured a story on them. It wasn't a huge deal, but little things like that along the way served to keep the momentum going and Blake involved with the industry. All of the talent involved in that particular venture went in different directions and each has had success in his or her own way.

The year 1996 was also when Larry and I moved to Franklin, just outside of Nashville. We had both taken early teachers' retirement in Oklahoma and sold our home there, along with much of our furniture. We lived with daughter Patti and David in Ada while we searched for jobs. In June, we moved to Williamson County, where Larry had attained a position as principal at Fairview and later Hillsboro in Leiper's Fork.

Especially during the first few months we were there, I wasn't working and Blake didn't have much going. Since it was a short drive from Nashville to Franklin, he was at our house a lot. He had a truck and he took me to pick up furniture as I finished furnishing the house. I didn't teach full time that first year, though I did do some substitute teaching in Fairview and worked part time with at-risk youth at My Friend's House in Franklin, helping teens with their studies. I remember coming home one day and Blake was teaching a few kids how to catch crawdads in the little stream near the community pool where we lived. They were all having fun, some of the little girls jumping back when he caught one.

Blake seemed happy to have us there. After a year and a half, Endy was almost ready to move back to Oklahoma, so the timing was perfect. I got him interested in a few word games like Scrabble and the noun game, a car game that we made up during trips back and forth to Ada. At first, I would let Blake win at Scrabble because I didn't want him to get frustrated and quit. I love the game but Larry doesn't. It wasn't long before Blake could win totally on his own merit. With the noun game, I'd usually start it with a noun and the next person would have to come up with a noun that began with the last letter of my noun, and so forth until one of us couldn't do it in a timely fashion: book, kangaroo, oven, napkin—you get the idea. The only problem was that Blake would always come up with a naughty noun and keep that up until he embarrassed me. If my noun was bat, he would counter with titty, that sort of thing—and it went downhill from there, a long way downhill pretty quickly once he got started. After a lot of that, I quit being embarrassed by much of anything he said. Besides the noun game, Larry would only play poker or blackjack. We kept a bag of pennies for our games and that entertained us a lot. Endy was still there for a while, but her job kept her busy and she actually had a social life. Blake really was too young for much of that as he still wasn't twenty-one. Since he hadn't grown up there, he didn't know anyone his own age. Mae Axton did call a couple of times asking if Blake would show some of her young relatives who were visiting around town and he did. He got good at driving in the big city!

When we moved to Franklin, we bought a home that was large enough for visitors, thinking a lot of family and friends would visit—and they did. The house had a large bonus room and we hosted many jam sessions there. Larry left his drums set up. Sometimes it was friends like Patty and Warren Kerckhoff; Rob and Rachel Byus; or Richard Mainegra, a songwriter for Elvis's "Separate Ways" (Red West, Mainegra), who had also been part of the group The Remingtons, but sometimes Blake brought people that were new to us. We always enjoyed the music!

Our house was big enough for me to have a dedicated office upstairs and I enjoyed sitting at my desk, which faced a window, allowing me to look out over the community while I taught myself to use a computer. (Patti would say that still hasn't happened.) I am known as a pretty organized person and I hang onto things, especially paperwork. There is an entire folder of handwritten songs in my file cabinet, a few which are dated. One titled "Can't Get It Together" was written by Karyn Rochelle and Blake on September 18, 1996. Some of them were written before that and some after; in the entire folder only three are actually dated. He wrote "Oklahoma" with Naomi Martin on November 15, 1994. And "The Last Country Song" is noted as being copyrighted in 1998 by Gosnell Music Group and SONY/ATV Music, written by Blake, Braddock, and Kosser. There are the lyrics to "That Old Frame (of was left out) Mine (mind)" by Charles Quillan and Blake. It was eventually titled "Frame of Mine" and featured in *Based on a True Story (Deluxe Version)* (2013) with lyrics almost the same as the handwritten version.

Also included in the folder was a list of songs Blake sang at the time along with the key for each, fifty-two in all. The list includes songs he had sung at the Music Palace like "Old Time Rock 'n' Roll" (Bob Seger and The Silver Bullet Band) and at the McSwain like "Shame Shame Shame" (Mark Collie), some he had written like "Fish Fry," and songs by the greats like George Strait's "The Fireman" (Mack Vickery, Wayne Kemp). It is full of variety! He was looking for his niche.

When Blake decided to get his songs a little more organized, I typed them all up and indexed them for him. It took a few days and he would sit in the corner and tell me how he wanted it done. I could type but a computer was relatively new to me, having bought my first one just prior to our move. In fact, Blake was the one who showed me how the little bar on the right would quickly move the page up or down. I had been hitting the arrows.

During our first year in Tennessee, we were constantly looking for things to do. Those days were relatively slow anyway, and I have snapshot memories of so many of the things we did when Blake was still full of dreams and expectations for his future. Once when Patti and David were there visiting, we played a round of miniature golf. He and Patti cut up through the entire game.

And one day, after we were through cataloging his newest songs, we started talking about Ada and I was telling him a little about its history. I told him about the historic hanging and decided to put "four men hanging" in the search bar to get even more information. When you do that today, the Ada story comes up immediately with pages of entries, but in 1996, what came up was a porn site (use your imagination here; it will be easy) and Blake burst into hysterical laughter. I felt sure the neighbors could hear him. With my lack of computer knowledge, I couldn't get that off the screen fast enough to suit me! That is the sort of thing he lives for!

On another day, he spotted something electronic-looking in the kitchen that he hadn't noticed before and asked about it. For Christmas the previous year, Patti had bought Larry a bird house that had a microphone in it so he could listen to the birds from a receiver in the house. I knew Blake liked anything that had to do with animals, so I showed it to him, and we accidentally tuned in to a baby monitor nearby. We couldn't resist listening to a lady talking and singing her baby to sleep but felt a little guilt at the unintentional intrusion on her privacy. Larry loved listening to the birds, so when the microphone quit working, I searched the internet for weeks trying to find a replacement with no luck. (I wonder if that is why they quit making them.)

One rainy weekend, Larry agreed to take a little trip to the Nashville Zoo. It was so wet we pretty much had the park to ourselves. I remember running from place to place in the light rain more than I remember the animals we saw there. Blake was mimicking the way I ran, kicking his legs back and up with each step, and I told him to enjoy since there would come a point that he couldn't roam about freely in public and act so stupid without being recognized. It seems I was always telling him that. I wonder if he believed it even a tiny bit. I did have an ulterior motive in that I felt it was important for him to soak up information about Nashville, since he was calling it home and should know a little something about the city and its surroundings. I don't think I can ever get too far away from the teacher in me.

Dorothy sent me a cute card just about that time and I still have it, thanking us for the help we had given Blake the past few years. She had drawn a picture of him on the side, complete with a cowboy hat and mullet. She drew a finger pointing to his ear with a note above the hand which read "still wet behind the ears." There was a pacifier and baby bottle on the side and a note below, "Take good care of him—he's just a baby! And Endy too!" I imagine it made her feel better to know that we were there keeping an eye out for them. I'm glad she took the time to send the card.

A slightly annoying memory I have is the time I tried to get him a job playing for one of our block parties in Buckingham Park but they turned him down. Really! I think I even offered to pay his fee which wouldn't have been much. He was there a lot and he would sometimes sit on the patio and sing. I guess they either hadn't heard him or didn't like his singing, although I can't imagine that. I bet some of those folks watch him on *The Voice* these days. But we loved Franklin, and Larry still talks about moving back. Every time we visit, it is like we never left. We always drive by our house and it seems like we should still be there.

Driving from our house toward Franklin Square, I had noticed a house that was painted in odd block shapes, predominately pink but each a different color. While gazing at that monstrosity one day, I saw a sign indicating Pinkerton Park. It looked like a good place to take our little dog, Jake, for a walk. Blake was willing to go, just something different to do. Pinkerton wasn't what it is today, and I don't remember any other people even being there. We just walked the paths and there were little plaques along the way that explained what had been there during the Civil War. I felt like we had stumbled upon a well-kept secret. It had been a Union camp, very interesting. After reading each little description of the area, it was easy to see where the soldiers kept their horses, made camp, and how they had built up areas for lookout points. There are so many hidden treasures in Franklin, Tennessee.

Just driving around new places was fun in itself. That's how we stumbled onto Fly, Tennessee, out in the middle of nowhere. And one day we decided to try to find Alan Jackson's home. He was my favorite singer and we were just out sightseeing anyway. I was giving Larry directions and he had finally located it and was driving very slowly when Blake caught Alan himself in the rearview mirror driving what I think was a Dodge Viper. Not wanting to look like a tourist, Blake and his 6'5" frame quickly disappeared beneath our car window. It was my turn to laugh at him. Like Alan Jackson would know who he was in 1996. Ha!

We loved having company and taking friends to see the Carter House, where families had holed up during the Battle of Franklin in 1864, bullet and cannon ball marks still easily visible, and Carnton Plantation, which had served as a hospital and burial ground. We went so often that they once asked Larry if he would like to participate in the reenactments. All our friends and family say that Larry is the best tour guide they've ever had.

We took Blake out to eat a lot. When we went to Cracker Barrel, he always ordered dumplings with a side of dumplings; we called it a white plate. At Demos in Nashville, he ordered fettuccine Alfredo, another white plate. And, when he cooked at home, his favorite was anything fried and he specialized in fried pickles. Of course, I always had M&Ms around and that didn't help either. He does eat healthier now, not that he has completely eliminated those foods from his diet. Once you've had fried pickles, you can't say you'll never try them again.

The score card from a round of miniature golf that the three of us played was dated September 4, 1996, with scores of Blake 41, Larry 36, and Carol 47, and commemorates a day of fun. Who knows why, but we each wrote a comment and signed the card. Larry's comment was, "Blake Shelton sadly took an ass whipping he will never forget!" Mine was, "I was too excited from Reba's party to really compete or I would have whipped them both. P.S. Also my feet hurt and cramp!" And finally, Blake's was, "Larry was led on to believe that Blake was really trying! Furthermore, the only person that can give ass whippings in this organization is *Blake Shelton!*" I think the party I referenced was the grand opening of Starstruck where Larry was the first to introduce Blake to Reba. I'm not sure Blake ever really believed he even knew her up until then.

Blake had always wanted a big aquarium, so being on his own, he got one. He didn't fill it with beautiful exotic fish but with a couple of catfish he had caught. I don't know where he caught them, but it was somewhere around Nashville. He did visit Percy Priest Dam on occasion and probably found a pond somewhere that had fish. One was unusual in that it was white. He kept them until they got so big that the aquarium simply would not hold them. I found a picture that had the aquarium in the background but it wasn't as big as I remember and the water was green. Those fish needed a new home. He was at a loss for what to do with them and finally came up with a plan, probably illegal. Very, very late one night, maybe even in the wee hours of morning, he put them in an ice chest filled with water, got Larry to help him carry it, and headed to the Opryland Hotel. There was a little stream flowing through it and they found a place with no people in sight and dumped the fish. For a long time after that, we would go and watch until we could spot that white catfish; finally, we couldn't find it and decided it was gone. I'm quite sure that today they would not have made it past the front door security carrying a heavy ice chest, but Blake just wanted to save the fish. His heart was in the right place. I don't know what Larry was thinking.

After Endy moved back to Oklahoma, Blake's steel guitar player Wayne Morton and his wife Susie moved into Blake's extra bedroom. It made it easier for the band to practice with Wayne there instead of Tishomingo, Oklahoma, where they lived, and he paid half the rent. Later, when it became obvious Blake couldn't afford a steel player, the Mortons moved back home. Still friends, Wayne is one of the guys Larry jams with in Ada every few months. And he is back in the band at the McSwain Theatre.

The year 1996 was a year of exploration, discovering new things about Nashville and Franklin, and learning about the city itself. I didn't think that Nashville embraced country music like it should. They liked the money it brought to town through tourism, but lacked a true appreciation for the art. When Planet Hollywood came to town, with lots of actors, people really turned out like the tourists they sometimes mocked. I like to believe that has changed now, partially due to the efforts of artists like Blake, Taylor Swift, and Carrie Underwood, who have successfully brought country music to mainstream audiences.

Appropriately enough, Blake ended the old year and began the new with three performances at Buffalo's in Stonewall, Oklahoma. His band at that time was called Road Kill. You just need one guess to know who came up with that. It was made up of Larry (drums), Luther Lewis (lead guitar), Craig Mosse (bass guitar), and Wayne Morton (steel guitar). Local fiddler Jeff Donaldson sometimes joined them for the shows in Oklahoma. Larry had always done an old rock 'n' roll medley, and Blake adopted it with his own version, something the crowd loved. A couple of times after he had gone out on the road full time, he got Larry up to do it with him at small clubs. More stories for Larry! Blake was also beginning to do some of his original stuff that maybe today he'd like to forget; songs like "Tex Is" and "Fish Fry." About that same time, local radio stations KADA and KYKC began playing those songs regularly. In fact, the winter newsletter in 1996 gave a shout-out to KADA and Roger Harris for continuing to be one of his most ardent supporters. (Years later, Larry was able to present Roger with a platinum album in appreciation of that early support.) Rich Kaye and Mike Manus, local Ada radio personalities, also loved to play Blake's stuff even way back then.

Returning to Ada for shows so often prompted a writer for the local newspaper to include in his column of predictions for the coming year that Blake Shelton would be returning to Ada to perform. It was a little sarcastic tongue-in-cheek comment with perceived implications that Blake would never really make it any bigger than that. Blake did not understand why anyone, especially someone from his home town, would say something like that, and I think it did hurt his feelings a little. Having never been a jealous person, he has always been supportive of all artists and never felt that bringing someone else down did anything to build himself up. This attitude came from his upbringing and Dick and Dorothy deserve all the credit for this important aspect of his personality. (It is what makes him such a great mentor to younger artists today and a breakout personality from *The Voice*.)

By this time, Blake was getting used to being on stage with a band. He didn't move around much but neither did George Strait, the guy he had chosen early on as a role model for his own career. He once said, "Can you imagine me hopping around up there with these long legs?" He laughingly called himself "Shufflin' Shelton" and he could do a rough moon walk with those big cowboy boots that made everyone laugh. But the serious side of Blake was ready to sign that record label deal and start working on his first album.

CHAPTER THREE

JUST GETTIN' STARTED

While we were back in Oklahoma for Christmas, my niece Mandy asked if she could return to Tennessee with us. She wanted to get away from where she grew up for a change. She followed us back and lived with us several months, working at a local O'Charley's restaurant, before moving back to Oklahoma. One night, Blake was there and wanted to go to night court in Nashville. Larry didn't want to go, so Blake said that if Mandy and I would, he would take us back to Franklin. It was probably the most entertainment outside of music I have ever witnessed in my life. It is no wonder that in the late 1980s and early 1990s, *Night Court* was such a popular situation comedy on television. The only difference was the television show didn't have the judge surrounded by bulletproof glass. I don't know why that didn't scare me off. There was a continuous stream of real-life characters brought into court for a variety of misdemeanors. My favorite was when one of them told the judge that he had his bail money at home if she would just let him go get it. She asked him if there was anyone in court that he knew and he replied affirmatively, that he knew John Doe (don't remember real name). She picked up a pen to write down some information and at that point, the policeman who had arrested him stepped forward to say that he was John Doe. The courtroom burst into laughter prompting a gavel from the judge.

There was also one obviously drunk man who was handcuffed and kept flirting with some girls from a local university crime class by winking and wiggling his hands around. Blake got a big kick out of that guy. He must have considered himself a ladies' man because he insisted on calling the female judge "Baby" and

49

she had to correct him every time. The three of us were fascinated by the humor in that strange setting and could barely remain solemn. Of course, Blake wanted us to laugh out loud so the judge would reprimand us but Mandy and I were afraid of her. When we got back home and told Larry what he had missed, we knew we were going back. When we did return a later night, Blake almost lost it when the bailiff literally yelled at Larry to "Take off that cap!" He had to duck down in his chair and hold his mouth closed to keep from laughing out loud. When we had visitors, we always took them to the Grand Ole Opry, Carnton Plantation, Carter House, and the Ryman. After those experiences, we added Nashville's night court to our tour.

Meanwhile, Blake never passed up an opportunity to write and sing. He and Rachel Proctor had written a couple of duets and had become a popular act at songwriters' nights in Franklin at Five Points Place and Henry's Coffeehouse in Nashville. They often got a standing ovation. Blake wasn't having luck at getting a recording contract and it was mentioned by someone that a duo might be a good idea. Brooks & Dunn had been around for a while and were dominating awards, so some insiders thought a new duo might make it easier to get recognition and award nominations. Blake and Rachel thought about it for a minute and made the decision to continue to go it alone, as solo acts. He continued to write with people like Rachel and Blue Miller and was enjoying making demos of his own music.

Since writing was a primary focus for Blake, I was always giving him song ideas that he never appreciated much. Once, he did use a title I found in a newspaper column, and he gave me writer's credit using my maiden name, Carol Cash (distant cousin to Johnny), though he never recorded it. It was called "Put You Out of My Misery." Since this is likely to be the only way it will see the light of day, and I only came up with the title so there's nothing to embarrass me, here are the lyrics penned by Blake:

Looks like the sun is comin' up on another cloudy day
I ain't seen a ray of hope since you went away
But I'll get up and spend my time layin' around in bed
'Cause you're already all inside my head
(CHORUS)
And I know that you're the reason
That my heart is freezin'
And why a long neck lasts a short time in my hands
And I know I'm gettin' lazy
And I'm goin' crazy
Doin' things that folks don't understand
And I don't even understand
Lord, I'm going nowhere fast
But slowly I'm beginning to see
That I've got to put you out of my misery
After a long day of thinkin' about the goodbye we never had
I'll pick up the phone and try to find out where you're at
Your mama says she just can't say 'cause you told her not to tell
But she's just adding fire to my hell
(CHORUS)

He sang it to me once and it had a beat to it like Don William's version of "Tulsa Time" (Danny Flowers), but that is all I can remember except that I was pretty excited about it at the time because it sounded good to me. Blake was happy with at least one line. He liked "And why a long neck lasts a short time in my hands."

In March, we scheduled the second annual fan club party at the Aldridge Hotel in Ada. It was always a good time to visit family and friends. While Blake was in town, he also made a visit to Ada High School and gave a presentation on the finer points of writing lyrics to Martha Nelson's creative writing class. He found it ironic because when he was in high school there were times he didn't think he would get through English, and now he was teaching the class.

A few months later when Mandy decided to return to Oklahoma, our daughter Debi (who had become disillusioned with her job in Sapulpa, Oklahoma) made the move to Tennessee, where she lived with us for a couple of years, long enough to become debt-free and able to buy a townhouse in Fairview, Tennessee. One memory she has is of Blake asking her, "When are you gonna get a job?" She quickly retorted, "When are you gonna get a record deal?" None of us are overly sensitive and he appreciated the humor in that. She did get a job as an advertising copywriter before he got his record deal, so she had the last laugh—for a couple of years anyway.

With both of them in Tennessee, most of the trips to Oklahoma included Blake and Debi and they always ganged up on me. On one trip, he figured out that if Debi had gotten married as young as I had (fifteen), she would be old enough to be his mother and I was old enough, by that math, to be his grandma. He got a big belly laugh out of that revelation.

And on that same trip, I was riding in front with Larry, and Blake was behind me. He had bought some Funyuns and was eating them and blowing his breath my way. I kept asking, "What is that smell?" He and Debi acted clueless and did that for hundreds of miles before I finally caught on to the trick. It did get him back in the front seat which was probably his goal in the first place. Blake was always fun to be around and the trips never failed to be entertaining. He enjoyed pointing out places with weird names like Toad Suck, Arkansas, or points of interest like Carroll County, Tennessee, which was memorialized in the Porter Wagoner classic, "The Carroll County Accident." On one trip that was just me and him, he taught me three chords (since forgotten) on a mandolin I had bought at school.

Those early road trips were always exciting because none of us had ever really been out of Oklahoma much. I don't remember exactly when it was, maybe when we went to Blake's showcase three years earlier, but we had a caravan going to Nashville. Blake and Dick were driving separate vehicles too, and Dick had hooked everyone up with CB radios so we could communicate. Everyone had a name. The only one I remember is Larry's. He was Buzzsaw. But at some point, Blake started back-talking a trucker and finally said something along the lines of "Pull it over big boy and I'll open up a can of whup-ass; I'm driving a white Chevrolet Suburban." (Blake was driving a blue pickup.) Larry, who was driving the Chevy, grabbed the microphone and straightened that out promptly! Blake has always been a hoot. He was continually going to "open up a can of whup-ass," and one time I asked him if he had ever been in a fight. He just laughed. I can't see him rolling around in the dirt. I can imagine there would have just been a lot of hair, arms, and legs.

No matter where we were, all of our time together was either doing something fun and silly or talking about Blake's career. The conversations just fluctuated back and forth. I am the world's best at changing the subject in the blink of an eye, and that always amused Blake. We could be having a serious discussion about something and I'd bring up something funny that had happened at school right in the middle of a sentence. Or we could be laughing and joking and I'd bring it down just as quickly with something dark. I don't possess a tenth of the focus he has.

Then came June and it proved to be a busy month for Blake. Of course there was another Fan Fair which was a repeat of the previous year, and that wouldn't change until he got a record released. He was continuing to build a fan base. Some showed up in his meet and greet line year after year despite no product out there, so he was there every year for the week-long event.

Immediately following Fan Fair, he headed back to Oklahoma where he wowed the crowd at the Oklahoma State Highway Patrol annual troopers' convention at Lake Texoma. They enjoyed him so much that he played an additional hour! It may not seem important today, but it was a self-esteem builder at the time.

But the biggest event for Blake that month was that he turned twenty-one! It did not go unnoticed as some of his closest friends and family met up in Tunica, Mississippi, for a weekend of fun and games. It was supposed to be a surprise but that didn't happen. We had thought we could tell him we would take him to Tunica since he was finally old enough to be carded, but he was too smart for us and figured it out. It was still a memorable event with Dorothy and Mike Shackleford, Dick Shelton and Terrie Delozier (Dick's future wife), Endy Shelton (who had moved back to Oklahoma), and Chuck Siess, Debi Large (who had joined us in Tennessee), Patti and David Binger (who had moved to Texas), Mike and Angie Stafford, Jim and Rita Sharp, and us. Debi has an iconic image in her mind of Blake sitting on a bar stool in front of a slot machine with his cap on backwards, a drink in his hand, and a cigar hanging out of his mouth. Blake really didn't have those vices, just part of the image he had of what he *could* do because he was now an adult. He was happy to be twenty-one. We hung out at Fitzgerald's and I still have the little leprechaun key ring with the card attached to track his winnings, although I doubt there was anything to track. The only birthday gift I remember him getting that he got a little excited about was a Vern Gosdin sticker for his guitar case.

Shortly after his birthday, he returned home for the Ada rodeo, where he got to be pulled out on that flatbed trailer to perform for the rodeo crowd and at the dance following, like so many music greats had done before. That had been a dream. It's kind of like the difference in playing the Ryman and playing the Grand Ole Opry. They are both great, but the rodeo *and* dance was the pinnacle of venues around Ada, Oklahoma. He had played a dance there but never both.

Then on November 29, his dad married Terrie Delozier. Performing during the reception at Wintersmith Lodge in Ada were Blake, Larry on drums, and Wayne Morton on steel guitar. Dick and Terrie took the first dance to the Garth Brooks classic, "The Dance" (Tony Arata). Blake and Endy realize how lucky they have been that their divorced parents got along well and were always supportive. In fact, Dorothy helped Terrie decorate their new home. Terrie would go on to finish her degree at ECU and become a teacher. She told me a few stories about Dick. One was when they were talking about their age difference and he had told her when he got too old to just tie him up to a tree and leave him. Years later, when he got sick, he asked her to not tie him to the tree just yet. He had hoped he would recover. I believe he did quit smoking. But after he passed and she was going through things, she found a note where he had written a slogan which read, "So let it be written, so let it be done, so sayeth the Dick." She said he would use this phrase from time to time when he wanted her to pay attention to what he had to say, adding that he was always coming up with funny stuff like that. He could tell a story such that you could not keep from laughing, often to the point of tears, as he shared memoirs from his days in the military. Our daughter, Debi, thought he was the funniest man she ever met.

And sadly, this was the year Blake lost his grandmother, Sammy Byrd, on December 9. Several of my friends in Ada remember Sammy bringing Blake and Endy to Dorothy's beauty salon after school when they were both young.

An exciting turn of events regarding his songwriting was when Blake signed a publishing deal with Gosnell Music. Michael Kosser was the president of the company and he and Blake had been writing together for over a year. They recorded a demo and Blake was beginning to feel like something was really going to happen. Blake and Michael also wrote "Ada, Oklahoma," and the Ada Chamber of Commerce adopted it as the city's song. While he was in Ada for a visit, he joined up with the Ada High School Choir for a benefit. He really did perform anywhere he was invited.

On March 28, 1998, Blake returned to Ada for his third and final annual fan club party to be held once more at the Aldridge Hotel. The song that got the most attention that year was one called "Only in a Honky Tonk," which he had cowritten with Ryan Murphey. The first line of the song mentioned Blake's Aunt Betty, and the crowd went wild. Susan Williams, of Gosnell Music Group, flew in to catch the fan club performance and brought her friend Paul Palmer Sr., who wrote a great review. He summed it up with "So here it is in a nutshell . . . you have got to see this artist and hear him for yourself to appreciate what I have to say next . . . world, get ready for Blake Shelton. He's going to treat you to a brand new sound and capture your hearts in the process! This guy is terrific!"

The party was followed by a performance at Buffalo's later that evening. Blake was starting to branch out a little more with his performances too, playing shows in Illinois, Louisiana, Texas, Tennessee, and Oklahoma.

Vernell Hackett (a nice lady I met while proofreading *American Songwriter* magazine as a side job) wrote an article in *Billboard* magazine about Nashville music publishing that mentioned Blake and included a picture of him. *Billboard* was going out to 110 countries and is considered the international newsweekly of music, video, and home entertainment. We were excited about every little thing that happened in regard to Blake on his rise to fame.

Blake was writing a lot. I had a list of seventeen new songs in his handwriting to add to his index. Unfortunately, I don't recognize even one of them today. But, it was important that he was honing those skills and once in a while, a favorite would surface.

Blake signed a production deal early in 1998 with Sony Tree Productions enabling him to do four demonstration songs, working with the legendary Bobby Braddock as his producer. Bobby heard of Blake through his friend Michael Kosser, who played him one of Blake's songs over the phone. Braddock wasn't blown away by the song but he was interested in the singer. Blake was over the moon excited about this new development. Not long before, a big time producer, who shall remain nameless, had shown interest in Blake but told him that he needed to start smoking so his voice would develop a more raspy sound. That was unacceptable to Dorothy, who never allowed him to smoke, to Larry, who swears he has never had a cigarette in his mouth, and to Mike and Angie Stafford, the doctor and nurse couple who were early supporters of Blake's music and knew it was a stupid idea. In fact, nobody was crazy about that guy's approach, no matter how much success he had as a producer.

Bobby Braddock was truly a godsend. Braddock, a Country Music Hall of Fame recipient, had been a prolific songwriter in Nashville for many years and had a slew of #1 songs. The one that almost everyone recognizes as the best country song of all time, "He Stopped Loving Her Today" by George Jones, was written by Braddock and Curly Putman. After he got a few songs recorded of Blake, Braddock took them to almost every label in town. The last label he went to was Giant because there was a rumor it was going to fold. It was a last ditch effort; however, they did offer a deal and it was accepted.

Blake signed his first major record deal in 1998 with Doug Johnson, president of Giant Records, achieving a major goal he had set for himself. In my book, that's equivalent to getting a college degree. Congrats Blake Shelton! You did it in four years!

Meanwhile, he turned in another ten songs to index and I still don't recognize any of them. But, in looking them over, there is one title that makes me really want to hear the entire song, "Big Hair Big Trouble." Anyway, I guess I can say he was working on his master's degree as he and Bobby began the long, arduous task of putting together his first album.

Concurrently, the internet was beginning to become really important to entertainers. A *Nashville.citysearch.com* site posted a comment about Blake under the title *The Next Garth* asking, "Where is the next monster male star? I'm here to tell you I have seen the future of country music and he is a young man now working steadily toward stardom. The guy has no flaws . . . He likes songs that tell a story, paint a picture, grab you by the imagination and hold on. I predict this kid will be a major star and that's no B.S. (clue)."

And the Blake Shelton Fan Club hopped on the information superhighway. I purchased blakeshelton.com, blakeshelton.org, and blakeshelton.net in an effort to protect his name as much as possible. My daughter Patti Binger bought a computer and began to learn how to build the first website. Always keeping Blake's image in mind, she researched and learned by trial and error to come up with something to make him proud. When the website went live, she received a voice mail from Blake saying, "Hey Patti, I just saw the website" and in a slow deliberate character voice added, "I-do-believe I have arrived!"

We were getting feedback from some of his team to make the website more technologically advanced, but we knew from talking to the fans that many of them only had dial-up internet or slow computers that could not handle advanced features. We finally compromised by doing a split screen with one side for dial-up and the other for DSL users. Also, many fans didn't have a computer at all, so we did a lot of snail mail promoting as well. Always brainstorming, we came up with *BSers* as a name for his fans and coined the phrase "Knee Deep in the Music" to describe Blake. Fans started using his name and initials in words at every opportunity. Blakeisms included "aBSolutely" and "blaketacular." Bobby Braddock kept us posted on what was new with Blake's music and was always complimentary to Patti and her work on the website. It was great that she got so much positive feedback, because she was doing it totally out of love.

Blake utilized almost every spare minute writing and recording. He considers himself fortunate to have been able to write in those early days with some of the greatest songwriters in Nashville: Bobby Braddock, Michael Kosser, Rachel Proctor, Phillip White, Richard Mainegra, Jimmy Melton, Neal Coty, Richard Fleming, and many others. That year he also recorded demos for Bill Anderson and Mark Collie. Blake and Rachel wrote a couple of duets that they demoed, which were heavily played on Ada radio.

He was staying pretty busy working toward his career, but he did date a little. Blake hadn't had a lot of experience cutting off a relationship so I really don't know why one girl became so upset.

But she showed up unannounced at his apartment and found him asleep in a recliner, put her face right in his and woke him up, scaring the hell out of him. Another one was even more memorable. I won't mention her name, but they didn't date long. I can only remember meeting her the one time when he brought her by our house and I took a picture of them, which I later threw away. She was unique in that she managed to get a guest spot on an MTV show with a popular band, and did they ever roast Blake! It was so much fun to watch her tell her story, and then members of the band would call him names and make fun of him. He got as much kick out of it as anyone. They never mentioned his name but we all knew it was him. I still laugh about it.

Then in November, Blake made an appearance at my school in Leiper's Fork as the opening performer for the Hillsboro Nights Concert Series benefitting Hillsboro School's music and arts program. Many stars supported Kids on Stage, a summer program brought to fruition by Aubrey Preston in 1996. Endorsed by people like Grammy winner Michael McDonald, the summer program, headed by Gene Cotton, has been extremely successful. One of Blake's musical idols, Mark Collie, was in the audience for the opening, and he would be returning in a few months for a concert of his own. Blake was a little nervous that night having Mark there and told the audience that he was in "Mark Collie land." After a brief intermission, he returned for more songs and had the crowd cheering him on, but he also had them in stitches as he told them how excited he was to meet his idol, so excited in fact that after he met Mark, he strolled into the girls' restroom to wash his hands, not realizing until later that he was in the girls' room and couldn't get the faucet to work. His excuse for the blunder: "I was still in Mark Collie land." Mark was another of Blake's early influences. At his showcase in 1994, he sang one of Mark's songs, "Let Her Go," and in the very first line, he could not find one of the notes. His voice wavered up and down and all around that note until he finally hit it and continued the song. Blake has a good ear and that must have driven him crazy, but the remainder of his show went well and the goof left us with a funny memory.

Everyone enjoys Blake's performances, great songs, and humorous stories. He has a unique voice, easy to distinguish, with his obviously country twang coupled with perfect diction and pitch, an unusual combination to be sure. I can't sing at all, but I can hear that I can't. I know how it is supposed to sound. I am always amazed at people who think they can sing when they are in fact pitiful. Once I asked Blake if he could feel in his throat when he hit a bad note, whether he could hear his own voice or not, and he said that he could. I think that is why he always sounds great live. He has never had to rely on special effects or tuners to make him sound good. Another thing that sets him apart is that, because you can always understand every word, you can truly appreciate the lyrics of the song as well as the melody. Everyone has a story of misunderstanding lyrics. I remember having an argument with twelve-year-old Debi once when "I Am Woman" by Helen Reddy was a big hit. Debi would always sing the main line that she was "invisible," and I finally corrected her that it was "invincible." I also told her what the word meant, but she wouldn't have it. She remembers me responding by saying something like "OK, remain ignorant." I'm sure she didn't hear it because she was unfamiliar with the word. But sometimes the cause is something else. For a while I could not get the song "Get Lucky," (Thomas Bangalter, Guy-Manuel de Homem-Christo, Nile Rodgers, Pharrell Williams) by Daft Punk and featuring Pharrell Williams, out of my head. I knew what I was hearing was not correct because no way were they singing "She's up on Mexican monkeys." Finally, I asked daughter Debi and learned it was simply "She's up all night to get lucky." Duh—the name of the song! But don't tell me it hasn't happened to you! Still, enunciation has never been a problem with Blake's vocals.

While Hillsboro Nights was clearly a G-rated audience, some of Blake's buddies (Bird, Buck, Corey, Robert) from Ada came to town to visit and wanted to hear Blake perform in a club. Larry convinced the manager at a famous bar on Broadway in downtown Nashville to give him an hour of stage time. Snapshots from that night reflect quite the party atmosphere and I don't think Blake thought there was anyone there who would be easily offended, certainly no children. There was a song floating around town published by Gary Secfton Music called "She'd Be a Perfect Lady (If She Didn't Say . . .)" and he decided to sing it and dedicate it to the guys. It is a hilariously funny song and everyone was laughing except the management, who asked Blake not to come back. I don't know if he has ever played in there since, but I bet they would have him back today with open arms. Words create strong feelings in people, some more than others. Once, after I was grown and had children, I slipped and said "shit" in front of my father, a rather dignified man who was a superintendent of schools, and he reprimanded me. I hated that I had said it in front of him, but I owned it and responded, "Oh Daddy, shit or shoo shoo, it's all the same stuff." He agreed but still wasn't happy. I also got called into the principal's office at Noble, Oklahoma, for using that word in the teachers' lounge. A friend turned me in! I made myself a curse jar at home and put a quarter in it every time the girls caught me using that word. They made a small fortune.

In late September, Blake attended his first *CMA Awards Show* watching Garth Brooks win Entertainer of the Year and George Strait take home the trophy for Male Vocalist of the Year. Those were big boots to fill, but Blake Shelton was working steadily toward doing just that.

By the time 1999 rolled around, Blake was becoming increasingly busy. We couldn't schedule a date for the fan club party during March at the Aldridge Hotel, as we had for the past three years. Having it there was almost like a family reunion for Blake because his immediate and most of his extended family lived around Ada. It ended up being a transitional year for parties that we wanted to continue but were obviously going to have to rethink.

IFCO had just initiated an internet chat room for artists and, since the party couldn't happen, we set it up for Blake to do one on March 27. We did it from our home in Franklin and Debi typed while Blake read and responded. It was pretty cool that fans from New Jersey, Pennsylvania, Florida, Oklahoma, Texas, Tennessee, and even Germany were able to join us through the miracle of cyberspace. Being in on the ground floor of the internet craze was an educational and exciting time. Setting up a chat room today would be no problem; people do it every day, but in the final years of the last century, it was far more challenging.

Meanwhile, Blake continued to write with other songwriters including Roger Murrah, Don Ellis, Billy Montana, and one of his great musical influences, Earl Thomas Conley. He was so excited to write with ETC that he drank tons of coffee that morning out of nervousness and by the time he arrived at Earl's house, the first thing he said was, "I need to go to the bathroom." Then he realized he was in Earl Thomas Conley's bathroom and it just felt so surreal to him.

Blake says he hasn't written many songs that he is really proud of but the one he wrote with ETC and Mike Pyle, "All Over Me," falls into that elite group. He always liked Dan Seal's falsetto in "Everything That Glitters Is Not Gold" (Bob McDill, Dan Seals) and this song offered that for him. When they got ready to record it, Blake invited Larry to the studio to observe. They had part of the Nashville Symphony there and he was fascinated with the process and the expertise with which Bobby Braddock orchestrated them so beautifully. Larry enjoys telling the story of how Bobby was able to hear one string, out of all those strings, that was out of tune and correct it before continuing with the recording. I believe it was the first time he met Bobby. Earl was there too and Larry remembers them all going to eat afterward. I thought I was there as well, but Larry assures me that I was not. Has he told the story so many times that I just think I was there or were there two different instances? It sure feels real to me; I can visualize a lady with a violin from a session. But I don't remember Earl or eating out afterward. An interesting side note that I have always found interesting is that Bobby Braddock, Dick Shelton, and Larry Large were all born within weeks of each other—and I don't know three men who had any bigger impact on Blake's life.

In June that year, Blake performed a show at Douglas Corner during Fan Fair festivities. He was introduced by Giant vice president Debbie Zavitson. It was really a showcase for the Giant label, as they had recently signed him and wanted to see him perform the new songs live. Several fans attended and it was sort of the unofficial live fan club party for the year, the beginning of the transition from March to June for the annual event. Blake would be performing in front of real fans as well as industry folks. Debbie Z was particularly important as she later found two of his biggest hits, "Austin" and "The Baby," and still later became his manager. Among the songs he sang that night were "Ol' Red" and "All Over Me."

It was at that show that our longtime Ada friends, Joe and Paula Stanford came to see Blake. They brought along their son, Stephen, who had just graduated high school. Stephen was so fascinated by all the musicians, fans, industry people—just the whole spectacle—that he kept calling his friend Mark Hardin, from Fittstown, Oklahoma, so he could enjoy the experience vicariously. Bag phones were the thing in those days and all the cool people, especially the guys, had one. I can remember Stephen running around with his and going outside around the corner where our cars were parked to make those calls to Mark. The kicker occurred when they got home and his dad got the phone bill the following month. Joe was, shall we say thrifty, unless he was the one doing the spending, and young Stephen had run up a bill of almost $400. Personally, I think the memory was well worth the money. And it did leave Joe with a good story.

Giant gave Blake access to the artists' area that year at Fan Fair and he took us with him. It was still outside at the fairgrounds back then. I happened to snap what would become my favorite picture ever of Blake on June 16, 1999. It was during that moment in time right between being nobody anyone knew and becoming a star. The backdrop is a packed crowd of fans watching the show from bleachers and a portable metal fence separating them from the artists. Blake is standing there watching the stage and wearing a small smile indicating a desire to be up there himself. What would become his image at least for the first few years, the early mullet and cowboy hat with a long sleeved shirt despite the hot day, was evident.

I must have written Dorothy about the prospect of becoming a famous mom because I have a card dated June 1999, where she talks about enjoying the visit she and Mike had with Blake on Mothers' Day. They got to meet everyone at Giant Records, went to the Grand Ole Opry, and met some stars and that Blake had said if they'd come back in July, they could watch him record. Then she ran out of room on the card and wrote on the inside envelope flap that she hoped I could read it, that she didn't know she was going to write so much. Then she sealed the envelope and wrote again on the outside of the back flap, "Oh—and no I can't wait to be a famous mom! I'm so proud of my baby." I'm glad I save little things like that; they are so much fun to look back on later.

Before the year was out, Blake was able to announce that he was working hard in the studio with Bobby Braddock and hoped to have his first album out by 2000. In November, Blake returned to the Hillsboro Nights Concert Series. He also played a benefit, alongside Giant label president Doug Johnson and Bobby Braddock, at Green's Grocery in Leiper's Fork, opening for Alan Jackson. Leiper's Fork is where I was teaching and Larry was assistant principal.

Blake's future was looking bright!

CHAPTER FOUR

NEON LIGHT

It has been reported that Blake and Kaynette (Katt) Williams were high school sweethearts, but that isn't exactly true. Blake was from Ada and she worked for Jerrell Newby at Jerrell's Photography in Ada when he was having high school senior pictures made. She was a pretty girl who liked hunting, fishing, and country music as much as he did. He ran into her again at the Ken Lance Sports Arena where they struck up a romance and she moved to Nashville. She was a math teacher at Leiper's Fork where I taught. They lived in Nashville a while before moving to a mobile home which was more in the country. When a strong storm blew through, it toppled a tree, which landed squarely on top of it and right through the roof. Both were lucky that they weren't hurt. They lived with us for a short while after that until they could relocate.

Blake rented a house that was big enough to accommodate having parties and they were able to host their own get-togethers. They often invited us and we were always by far the oldest ones there. It never seemed to bother them or their friends and the parties were always fun. One guy showed me his nipple rings at one, not something that ever occurred at one of our own parties. And there were special moments as well. At one of those parties, Joe Nichols sat and played me several songs. He was a quiet guy with a beautiful voice and he was one of the nicest performers I ever met. Blake and I talked about him right after that. He agreed that Joe was a huge talent and couldn't understand why he wasn't already a superstar. I told him I thought it was because his genuineness didn't come across in big venues like it did in smaller ones. Of course, I am a country music fan and like all of us, have my opinion. Everyone knows what they say about opinions, but I loved listening to Joe sing and am happy for his success.

Meanwhile, our little group always found things to do and although none of us were bowlers, we decided to give that a try one night. The game was on! I don't know if Larry was just clumsy or maybe the holes in the bowling ball were too small for his big fingers, but when he started to throw it down the lane, it didn't release and the momentum sent him and the ball into the gutter. Of course, we all cracked up at that spectacle. Richard Mainegra was the only one who even checked to see if he was OK. The rest of us were doubled over with laughter! This is Blake's kind of humor and it rubbed off, that laugh when your friend (or husband) makes a fool of himself in public. It was a slip-on-a-banana-peel moment I'll never forget.

Blake was well settled in Tennessee, but Ada, Oklahoma, had not forgotten him either. On December 31, 1999, area residents placed items in a time capsule and buried it on the Pontotoc County Courthouse lawn, to be opened in 2100. Tucked into the vault with thirty-eight other items listed was #28, "Ada, Oklahoma," a song on cassette tape by Blake Shelton, donated by the Ada Area Chamber of Commerce. Thinking about it now, they probably should have included a tape player as well.

Many thought that at midnight December 31, 1999, computers would crash and the world as we knew it would come to an end, but it did not. Life went on as usual. Blake began the new millennium with some new goals: perform at the Ryman, release his first single and album, and get out on the road to perform more. In late February, he had his first opportunity to perform at the Ryman along with Jo Dee Messina and other new artists during Nashville's Radio Seminar Week. It was an opportunity for him to meet radio personalities from across the nation at that major event before actually going out on his radio tour to publicize his first release. Another highlight that week was a special In the Round concert with Neal McCoy, Georgia Middleman, and the Wilkinsons.

He was also spotlighted at another annual event in Nashville. Every year the Screen Actors Guild (SAG) and American Federation of Television and Recording Artists (AFTRA) sponsored a Block Party on Music Row in Nashville. That year Blake Shelton represented Giant Records by performing two songs from his promotional CD. "All Over Me" was the song he had written with Earl Thomas Conley and Michael Pyle, and "Ol' Red" was the one Hoyt Axton sang to him on his bus back in 1994. What could have been more Nashville than singing at an event hosted by the colorful Porter Wagoner, who was the inspiration for Dolly Parton's mega hit, "I Will Always Love You"?

Larry was anxious for Blake to get a bus and get out on the road, and they had decided he would be the merchandise manager when that happened. Upon retirement in April 2000, Hillsboro Elementary/Middle School threw Larry a big going-away party. Every class (K–8) did something special. There were decorated tee shirts, pictures, poems, and songs just for him. Blake was there and sang too. He had been a fixture at Leiper's Fork, performing for Kids on Stage and showing up sometimes unexpectedly. Larry was putting the cart before the horse, so to speak (or the road gigs before the radio tour), and he ultimately had to return to work in the fall as interim assistant principal at Page High School in Williamson County.

End-of-the-year school activities kept us busy but we still managed to organize a fan club party that June at one of our favorite venues, the Douglas Corner Café. It had a cozy atmosphere and was packed with fans and industry people who loved Blake and his unique style and personality. It had been around since 1987 and had witnessed label showcases for many artists, including Garth Brooks, Alan Jackson, and Blake Shelton, along with many others. It was also the setting for Keith Whitley's video, "I'm No Stranger to the Rain" (Sonny Curtis, Ron Hellard). Mervyn Louque, owner and sound engineer, was always congenial and had a list as long as your arm of great acts he had recorded. On a side note of unique

Nashville trivia, Mervyn was married to Jennifer O'Neill, actress from *Summer of '42.*

That was also the year Blake's sister, Endy, designed some awards for us (me, Larry, Debi, Patti) and presented them at the party. Blake posed with us for a couple of snapshots. They are interesting because the girls and I are well over a foot shorter than Blake and even Larry is barely above his shoulders. We all sported big smiles. Patti and David lived in Texas but always managed the drive to Tennessee for fan club events.

We enjoyed very much the years Blake sang at Douglas Corner. It was quite close to Berry Road where he first lived in Nashville. Of course he also attended other events that week; signed autographs at *American Songwriter*, *Country Weekly*, and the Ernest Tubb booths; and performed at the IFCO evening show with Charlie Daniels, Eric Heatherly, John Berry, Paul Overstreet, Lynn Anderson, and others. Paul Overstreet was another artist that Blake admired. It was his song "If I Could Bottle This Up" (Overstreet, Dean Dillon) that Blake sang when he won Oklahoma's Denbo Diamond Award years earlier as a sixteen-year-old from Ada.

Right after Fan Fair week, Blake performed a Listener Appreciation Show in Saginaw, Michigan. He enjoyed a couple of performances at the Bluebird Café and Matthew Gilliam continued to feature him on the *WSM Opry Spotlight Show*. When I tagged along, I took Matthew homemade cookies so I quickly became his friend. During one interview, he was raving about Blake's new website and ended up calling Patti. He told her to grab a pen and write down his phone number and call him back. She did and when he got her on the air, he asked her "Does Blake pay you a lot of money for doing his website?" Patti didn't miss a beat and replied, "Blake doesn't pay me enough money to buy that pen I needed to write down your number!" Matthew enjoyed that quip and kept her live on air for quite a while, until she started plugging an upcoming Joan Jett appearance in Nashville. That caused Blake to yell, "*Hey!* This is about *me!*" and the interview was over. Matthew always encouraged Blake to play and sing anything he wanted, including a few songs that would never gain airplay otherwise. It was always fun for Blake to do that. Early in his own career, he appreciated the importance of the artists and music that came before him as well as recognizing that the genre was evolving.

Everything was progressing pretty well. Blake was offered endorsements from Wrangler and Takamine. At that time Blake wore nothing but Wranglers and had been playing a Takamine since his teen years, so they were both a good fit for him. Edyie Brooks Bryant of Wrangler was always great to us during Fan Fair and our parties by giving fans everything from jeans to sunglasses. She has remained a friend through the years. I remember there were two giant posters of Blake wearing Wranglers on each side of the entry to the exhibition hall at the CMA Festival. Every little thing like that made me realize that his popularity was steadily increasing. What was not to like about Blake? He was and is genuine. He loves people, loves hearing their stories, loves entertaining them. During his first few years in Nashville, it did not bother him one bit to give anyone and everyone a big hug. I think some of the professionals were taken aback by it at first, but soon they recognized that it was part of his personality. The Blake you see on television is the Blake you would see if you were sitting with him in his living room.

Just before he headed out for his radio tour on October 30, 2000, he performed a show at the Douglas Corner Café. We were excited that Larry's cousin Farrell Large and wife Sue were in town and able to attend that one. When we made the move to Nashville, almost everyone thought we were crazy. Farrell and Sue were encouraging and it was refreshing.

Blake has always been great with people and the radio tour enabled him to make a lot of new friends across the country. Radio DJs loved him because he was funny and easy to interview. He showed his salty sense of humor and knew when (usually) to draw the line. He hugged them, kissed them, licked their faces, stuck his finger in their ears; you name it, he did it. He was memorable and in addition to all that, the boy could play a pretty mean acoustic guitar to accompany himself on songs that he belted out with ability and assurance. "Austin" (David Kent, Kirsti Manna) was being heard from coast to coast and would soon begin to climb the charts.

Meanwhile, knowing his fans were disappointed that the single didn't come out in time for Christmas 2000, Blake came by the house one day with a big box full of music and I sent every fan club member a CD of two songs, "Problems at Home" (Blake Shelton, Billy Montana, Don Ellis) and "Same Old Song" (Bobby Braddock).

The new year, 2001, brought hopes that a single would finally be released. Blake's goal at that time was to simply get a song into the top 10 in *Billboard*. He seemed to be on repeat as he again performed live on WSM-AM from the Ernest Tubb Record Shop and also at the Ryman during the Country Radio Seminar along with John Michael Montgomery, Lila McCann, Hal Ketchum, Chalee Tennison, South 65, and Christi Sutherland. Blake got a big laugh from the audience when he welcomed radio seminar guests and fans alike to his "second annual debut" at the Ryman. He had been a crowd favorite the year before and everyone expected to hear him on the radio in 2001. But the wheels do move slowly, and he had gone back into the studio.

Blake and Bobby Braddock had been working feverishly writing, recording, selecting, and discarding songs for that important first album. At about the time they were finishing it up, Debbie Zavitson, vice president of A&R at Giant, found a song that she thought would be perfect for Blake. I remember like it was yesterday—Blake calling me in the wee hours of the morning and singing a song he was so excited about that it couldn't wait until the next day. It was "Austin." Thinking back, he must have been working all evening on his own guitar version. According to Braddock, the first time he heard the song, Blake wasn't overwhelmed by its piano accompaniment, but he was encouraged by the label to take it home and practice it with his guitar. That changed everything for him. I don't know which other song bit the dust for "Austin" to make it onto the album, but it was very late in the game. And, then it was decided it would be the first single from the album. Originally "If This Is Austin," Braddock convinced Blake and the label that it should be shortened to the simpler title, "Austin."

Blake acknowledges Fritz Kuhlman (a promotion guy who knew Giant was going to close) for what happened next. Kuhlman had them print up "Austin" a couple of months ahead of the scheduled release date and quickly sent copies to radio stations, who immediately began playing it. Due to that timing, Blake had a chart-climbing single when the label actually folded on Friday, April 13, 2001. That's right—Friday the 13th!

As they were closing up shop, I remember Blake bringing home a huge box of various CDs that were headed to the trash before he saved them. Irving Azoff had initially co-owned Giant with Warner Bros., who agreed to purchase the remaining shares. They temporarily took all the artists with them to their label, but it was known that most would be cut.

Without a label continuing to promote it, "Austin" would persevere and spend five weeks at the top spot, tying the record held by Billy Ray Cyrus's "Achy Breaky Heart" (Don Von Tress). That's all it took to convince Warner Bros. to bring Blake Shelton on board. We had all been on pins and needles until Warner Bros. picked up the single and the album and continued to support Blake as they do to this day. It couldn't have happened without a killer song and the nudge given it by Kuhlman.

Thank you Debbie Zavitson! Thank you Fritz Kuhlman!

Larry and I had been calling in radio requests for it constantly, trying to change our voices each time. Blake watched us do it and just laughed at us. Of course, that didn't make a dent in the success of the song as fans from across the nation were doing the same thing and they didn't know Blake Shelton. There was such a debate from fans on whether Austin was a girl or the city; I can't help thinking it was a topic of conversation at water coolers all over America. I spent hours online at his website answering the question with, "Maybe both."

I didn't know the actual story at the time, but Blake explained it to Tom Roland in an interview for *The Tennessean.* "I'll tell you who would leave a message like that on their machine. It's a guy named Ash Underwood that lives in Nashville." He went on to explain that Underwood's girlfriend moved to Austin, and he tagged his outgoing messages with a profession of his love. Songwriter David Kent called his house one day and thought the message was the basis for a song. He asked Underwood to help him write it. When Underwood said no, Kent turned to Kirsti Manna to cowrite it. As it turned out, Underwood risked getting robbed by leaving his schedule on his answering machine, turned down an opportunity to collaborate on a lucrative hit song, and (unlike the song's happy ending) didn't even get the girl.

Second to the Austin query, our most frequently asked question was, "Is Ricky Van Shelton Blake's father?" Blake only encouraged the confusion by answering "Yes!" about half the time. As a point of clarification, there is no relation between Blake and Ricky.

During all the excitement of the song rising on the charts and the label closing, Blake continued to work hard, singing for Don Ellis's celebrity golf tournament benefiting Special Olympics and at Oklahoma's CountryFest among others.

On May 5, 2001, and grinning from ear to ear, Blake turned an important corner in his career. He made his first appearance on the Grand Ole Opry. Just one look at him as he took the stage, first from Porter Wagoner and later from Bill Anderson, you could tell that Blake was in his element. He was so excited to be on that stage and to stand in that circle where so many had stood. In fact, he took a couple of seconds to just walk around the circle. The audience loved his enthusiasm and his music. Of course, he sang "Austin," which was becoming well known, and another song, "That's

What I Call Home" (Richard Mainegra, Blake Shelton, Michael Kosser), from the yet-to-be-released album.

The Opry was a lifetime moment for Blake, to be in the backstage company of Billy Walker, Jeannie Seely, Jack Green, Connie Smith, Little Jimmy Dickens, George Hamilton IV, and others. Daughter Debi took a picture of Blake on stage singing that night that sits in my home office today. He wore a dull gold-colored shirt tucked into faded blue Wranglers with a brown western-style belt and silver buckle. With his black felt hat and cowboy boots (though you can't see them in the picture), and playing his shiny black Takamine guitar held up by a simple black guitar strap, he stood there singing his heart out. That is the Blake Shelton early fans like Connie Schultz still remember. Connie has followed Blake's career relentlessly and when I have a question, it is her I call. It's too bad she wasn't there that night. I was as excited as Blake to be backstage and in awe of all the performers I had come to know through the years on television—and some from Larry's days at the Ken Lance Sports Arena.

Jeannie Seely fascinated me. Something came up about guest rooms and she said, "I don't have a guest room; I found that it attracted guests." I do not know why it struck me so funny that I still remember it after all these years, but it just did. What Blake remembers is that he sang "Austin" and that he knew it was his shot at selling the song, because people could hear it live from coast to coast on the radio.

Blake was also setting up a new band and getting ready to go out on the road. Larry agreed with the label that he should get younger guys and they were holding auditions. One young man came in to try out for drummer. He was a good drummer but he had been playing other genres and wasn't getting the feel of country music. Blake asked Larry to play a little bit of the song and he did. It was obvious he was happier with Larry's licks. Later, Blake laughed about what that guy must have thought that he could just call up someone sitting there watching to show him how to play. He finally did hire a drummer, David Spak, and got his band ready for the road. I'm thinking nobody liked any band names he came up with based on his earlier choice, Road Kill, so the band remained nameless. We continued the tradition of a party at Douglas Corner, but it was beginning to get too small to accommodate everyone, so we knew we would have to start looking around for a bigger venue.

Blake was getting into commercials a little, doing a couple of regional ads for Ford Trucks. Ford guys Clifford and Charles Lambreth were also good to the fan club, donating things like a leather jacket and other items to give away at the party. And the video for "Austin," directed by Deaton-Flanigen Productions and filmed after the song had reached the top 10, was being played often on Country Music Television (CMT) and Great American Country (GAC).

Blake also performed at the 34th Annual IFCO Fun Fest show along with the Bellamy Brothers, Keith Urban, Paul Overstreet, and many others, in addition to signing in the exhibit hall at CMA's Fan Fest.

In June 2001, with a new band, a hit, and a self-titled album in the works, Blake Shelton was hitting the road. He couldn't have been any more excited than Larry to be actually getting out there. The only current band member who was with him then was bass player Rob Byus. At that time Rob was married to Rachel Proctor, who had a history writing and singing with Blake and also accompanied them and performed at some of the shows.

Blake has admitted that his sudden popularity messed with his head a bit and that there's a lot of temptation out there. He was learning how tough it was to be out on the road. I tried to get him to read the Travis Tritt autobiography, *Ten Foot Tall and Bulletproof*, but there was no chance of that. We all thank God that he made it through those tough years and has managed to remain the Blake Shelton we have always known.

He was scheduled for another Opry performance on Saturday, June 30, 2001, and the show was dedicated to Chet Atkins, who had passed earlier that day. He would quickly follow with performances on July 13 and again on the 14th, actually singing on the live televised portion of the show. The Grand Ole Opry was a giant goal he had set for himself. Stop and think how this twenty-five-year-old Oklahoma boy (yes, boy) felt, how Larry and I felt, and how all his family and friends back home felt as well. "Proud" simply isn't a strong enough word!

His third appearance on the Opry happened to coincide with a special Mayberry Reunion featuring the actors who portrayed Barney Fife, Thelma Lou, Ernest T. Bass, Malcolm the Butler, the Darlins, and others. They were guests of the Grand Ole Opry and were all hanging out backstage.

Mayberry reminds me of a story Larry shared with me when I asked him to give me some road stories. He said he mainly remembers a stinky bus with at least ten guys and one girl driver, Valerie Wren. Everyone, including Blake, slept in a bunk. There was a small room at the back meant as private quarters for the star. Blake chose to use it as a place where they could watch television or play video games as pastime on the long trips. Spak was the drummer and when he changed drum heads, he got everyone to sign them and Larry would sell them in the merchandise booth. I still have one I actually bought for $20. The money went into a kitty so they could purchase new games and television videos. One of the collections was *The Andy Griffith Show*. So it was fun to meet those characters from their favorite show. Of course, it is well known that Blake loved *The Golden Girls*, but I don't think he was ever able to win enough votes to buy that series. The fact that his favorite was the character Dorothy (Bea Arthur) explains a lot about Blake's sense of humor.

The Opry was always important, but Blake's dad was especially excited when he learned that Blake had been asked to sing the National Anthem at Talladega (NASCAR event). When Dick learned that Blake would be performing at this event, he told him to clear a bunk because he was going. He met Richard Petty, got a picture with him, and enjoyed the race. What Larry remembers about that is just before he started to sing, Blake turned to him and said, "What is the first line?" He was joking but Larry was petrified for him. And he did sing one line twice but unless you were singing along with him, you would not have noticed.

July 31, 2001, was the day all the stars aligned for Blake Shelton. He was in Ada, Oklahoma, to meet fans, friends, and family at Hastings Book Store. Mayor Amelda McCortney declared the day Blake Shelton Day. His first album, *Blake Shelton,* was released that day. And "Austin" went to #1 on record charts that day! Warner Bros. called him but he couldn't get reception inside Dorothy's house on South Broadway Boulevard, so he went outside and was standing in the driveway when he got the news. There would be celebrating that night!

Someone brought a copy of the local front page news, and Patti snapped a picture of Blake holding up the paper. It was a fun and exciting day. Hoyt's sister-in-law, Martha Axton, lived in Ada and she brought Blake one of Hoyt Axton's suede jackets. Tony Pippin (*Ada Evening News*), who had covered Blake's career for years, couldn't have been happier with the day's news and that the self-titled album, *Blake Shelton*, hit #3 on the *Billboard* Top Country Albums chart. Four of the songs were written or cowritten by Blake.

In August, Blake appeared on the cover of *Music Row's Twentieth Anniversary Collector's Edition*, one of my all-time favorite covers. At twenty-five, he still had somewhat of a baby face; his hair was still long but the photographer managed to blend it into the shading of his tan suede jacket. He was wearing a dull gold shirt with the top button undone and a white cowboy hat with a narrow black headband, accented with two silver metal diamond shaped studs flanking a center strip of tan. Sideburns came down to the bottom of his ears but again, they were somewhat in the shadow, making the picture timeless. What catches one's attention first, though, were his blue eyes. His blue eyes and beautifully sincere smile are definitely his best physical features.

Later that month, Warner Bros. hosted a #1 party to celebrate the success of "Austin." Blake invited us, but I didn't really know anyone except him and sort of wandered around aimlessly while Larry socialized until the presentations began. They were giving everyone associated with the song giant Bugs Bunny stuffed animals and they looked kind of funny lined up on that stage with them. There were giant foam hands with #1 printed on them and I kept one of those for years until it disintegrated. Nashville was buzzing about Blake and he was on cloud nine.

There was a huge billboard of the album cover at the corner of Broadway and West End in Nashville. Debi drove down there one day on her lunch hour to get a snapshot of it. And Tower Records on West End had a giant poster of him at the front door. Blake went in there and asked one of the young clerks, "Who is that guy anyway? Is he any good?" When Blake wasn't on stage, he usually wore tennis shoes, jeans with a tee shirt hanging out, and a baseball cap. And he tended to slump. He once said to me, "I have the posture of a vulture, don't I?" Well, yes, sometimes he did. I guess he was trying to get down to everyone else's level, and it became a habit he was trying to break. Anyway, I don't know if the clerk recognized him or not, maybe not.

It was an exciting time, and I kept reminding Blake to enjoy every second of it. Of course I used to tell him that very early on, too. I wanted him to recognize that it was important to remember those things so he could truly appreciate the successes. And I think he did. At that same time, Larry was getting excited to go on the road with Blake as merchandise manager. He wanted Blake to hold on to his own merchandise as long as he could so that when and if he did sell it, it would be worth more.

Blake's first big award nomination was in 2001 by the Academy of Country Music. He got the nod for Top New Male Vocalist in

2001 and 2002, followed by a nomination for the Vocal Event of the Year, "The Truth About Men" (with Tracy Byrd, Andy Griggs, and Montgomery Gentry) in 2003. The song had been written by one of his early influences, Paul Overstreet, along with Rory Feek and Tim Johnson. The Country Music Association nominated him for the Horizon Award that year as well. He didn't grab a win in any of those early categories, and it would be 2010 before he started taking any awards home with him. The important thing was that Blake Shelton was beginning to be noticed by more and more people. His name was still unknown to many but almost everyone recognized his song, "Austin."

Following a gig in Florida, Blake noticed a karaoke bar across the street and headed over there. Larry said he was excited to discover that "Austin" was a choice. He sang it and while the patrons applauded, nobody appeared to recognize him. Blake thought that was pretty cool.

Larry also tells the story of when he played an outdoor venue in the Midwest. They could look up and see the mountains and actually see a huge cave up there. Blake and Larry decided to climb up there for a closer look. Larry said it was a pretty steep slope up that mountain and he was struggling with loose rocks and hanging on to scrub brush as they made the ascent. Blake, having longer legs and youth on his side, got up there far quicker than Larry did, went in the cave and came back out yelling at Larry to "Come on; there are cave drawings in here!" Larry loves that kind of thing, which Blake obviously knew, and he rushed to get up there to see. When he went in, he could see a drawing all right, but it hadn't been drawn by an unknown artist hundreds of years ago as he had hoped. The quickly scratched out obscene drawing had been there a minute or two, artist known. Larry said they could hear Blake's laughter from the bus at the bottom of the hill and probably farther as it echoed through the mountains.

Blake remembers the first time he was recognized in public. It was at Hardee's, somewhere between Kansas City and Manhattan,

Kansas. He went in to get a hamburger and a young guy and his wife walked up to him and asked, "Are you Blake Shelton?" He had to admit that it was a good feeling to be recognized but probably meant he should straighten up a little bit in public.

He was touring coast to coast with Lonestar, and he got to open for George Jones a time or two. George introduced him as Blake *Skelton* once and he loved it, but Nancy Jones straightened George out on the name. In a moment of chivalry, Blake helped me locate a good seat in the dark at one of those shows.

He had already started working on his second album with producer Bobby Braddock. When he was ready to record "Playboys of the Southwestern World" (Neal Coty, Randy VanWarmer), he wanted background sounds of partygoers. He needed to look no further than Blake and his buddies. Longtime friend, Patty Kerckhoff, remembered to take a camera and when I look at that picture, I can spot Braddock's daughter Lauren, who has since become a friend, and her husband, Jim Havey; my teaching buddy and her husband, Stacy and Bryan Huddleston; and Patty's husband, Warren. I was sick as a dog that night but I wouldn't have missed it for anything. Oh, and I can't sing a lick, but I definitely could pull off a drunk sounding partygoer.

"All Over Me" was released as the second single in October but only made it to #18, such a disappointment. It is one of those songs you should find and give a listen if you are a fan of Blake Shelton's music.

Blake got the opportunity to be a part of *Opry Family Reunion*, a concert filmed by producers of *Country's Family Reunion* and Gaylord Entertainment. The participants, made up of mostly Opry members and a few newcomers, were seated in a circle on the stage of the Ryman. The eight-volume video set was released in October and coincided with the Opry's seventy-sixth anniversary. The seasoned veterans seemed to especially love Blake's version of "Ol' Red" (James "Bo" Bohan, Don Goodman, Mark Sherrill) as well as "Austin." It was an honor for him to be included in a project with so many illustrious country stars. He was beginning to feel like part of the country music family, but he still sat at the kids' table.

Finally Blake, tired of renting and with the money he had earned through the success of "Austin," bought his first home, a modest farm in Centerville, Tennessee, home of Minnie Pearl. I don't know why he moved around so much; he was unconsciously looking for a place that reminded him of Oklahoma, I suspect. He seemed to keep getting farther away from the city with every move. What made this a little different was that he was putting down roots with the actual purchase of the farm.

He was proud of that first home which came with 460 acres as well. He made a few improvements himself, painting the walls and little things like that. It was small. When Dick and Terrie came to visit, they had to eat on TV trays because there wasn't room for a table. There was another old house on the property and he offered to let us stay there rent free, but I was pretty happy where we were and it would have required some work. Blake later added a room and a huge deck so he could enjoy outdoor living. He also built some ponds and planted a few crops.

Blake decided a farm needed animals, so he bought fifteen ducks, sixty chickens, twenty hogs, and a pet turkey named Turkey. He once joked that he enjoyed "feeding Turkey turkey." I can't verify the truth in that quote. Once, while he was out on the property hunting, two mud-covered mutts wandered out of the woods. He took them home, cleaned them up, and named them Austin and Ol' Red. He said his farm was "like a bad episode of *Green Acres*." But he got a tractor and some other farm equipment and was enjoying learning to be a farmer. He even talked of getting cows in the future.

Their neighbor, who happened to be an assistant deputy sheriff, had some unique goats. Blake tried to scare them away one day by shooting his gun into the air. What he didn't know was that they were myotonic (fainting) goats. When those goats are frightened, their muscles freeze for about three seconds and they collapse.

He thought he had killed them and he knew who owned them so thought he had really, as he loved to say, "screwed the pooch."

Blake was branching out with his road tour, playing all over. On December 9, 2001, he played Splitfire in Vacaville, California. I have a card from that event showing ticket prices of $15 or $30—if you wanted to have dinner *and* the show. Today, that wouldn't get you into a movie with popcorn and a soft drink.

I'm not sure exactly when it happened, but around this time, Blake changed managers. Blake had met songwriter Michael Kosser through his first manager, Jim Sharp, and Bobby Braddock through Kosser, who wrote articles for Sharp's magazine, *American Songwriter*.

Moving on, Blake hired Debbie Zavitson, who was responsible for finding his first two #1 hits. She had moved up the ranks at Giant and he had planned to hire her as his new manager even before the label folded. I had always been impressed with Pam Lewis who, along with Bob Doyle, managed Garth Brooks when he first started, and I thought a woman might just work harder.

I really liked Debbie Zavitson, mainly because she believed in Blake, felt his voice was sincere, and recognized that he was well liked by everyone who met him. She soon asked John Dorris Sr. to join her as comanager, probably because she recognized that he had more experience in that field. Eventually, she went back to her true love of songs and songwriters, but she was a crucial part of Blake's success. Dorris continued to manage Blake's career until 2005, when he signed with Starstruck Management. John remains one of my favorite storytellers ever!

Trivia for 2002 included the fact that Blake got to meet Chubby Checker at the Country Radio Seminar in February, and we moved the fan club party to the Hard Rock Café in downtown Nashville in June.

The party was a breakfast and fans liked it so much that we continued that time frame for a few years afterward. However, it was obvious that the venue was going to be too small. Blake's fan-base was growing daily. He always had so much fun interacting with them and many still follow him. He remembers most of them. Occasionally, he will ask, "What is Crazy Connie (Slater) doing these days?" or "Do you still talk to those Birthday Girls?" At the party that year, Blake declared to *Country Weekly*, "These fans are taking time out of their lives to spend two hours with me, and all they want in return is an autograph! It's awesome." He roamed around while they were eating breakfast, visiting with them, and later did an acoustic set, which was always special. That was the first year media had asked to come to the party and we were so happy that Blake's party had reached that level of interest.

There was a time that his fan club membership fell below one hundred, but I never told Blake. Later, of those people who continued to stay, and most did, we created the 89ers and they became lifetime members. That was when dues were attached to memberships, but those eighty-nine will always remain special in our hearts.

Newsletters went full-color, which was exciting for us behind the scenes. Blake always liked any improvements. He appreciated that his fans were among the best treated in all of country music. She is my daughter, but I have to say that Patti Binger did an excellent job with that website at a time when many artists didn't even have one. Blake actually recommended her to a new artist, but she said that running his site was a full time job and she would remain committed to it alone.

In February, Blake went into the studio to cut some new songs. He wasn't in a big hurry for the next album, realizing it took three years to make the first one. He was starting to understand that while he considered himself the luckiest guy in the world to get to do what he was doing, it was a lot of work.

Something happened that year that really got Patti aggravated. I think it started at the annual Block Party in Nashville, but when it continued in an interview, it put a bee in her bonnet that she hasn't

Winning Oklahoma's Denbo Diamond Award, 1992. PHOTO BY ANGELA STAFFORD

Accepting congratulations from Mike and Angie Stafford. PHOTO BY ANGELA STAFFORD

Larry and Blake waiting for first flight to Nashville.

Graduation from Ada High School, 1994.

Blake with his family, Endy, Dorothy, and Dick displaying a pair of Willie Nelson's tennis shoes donated to Blake's fan club for a benefit.

Me and Blake during rehearsal for a show at the Pontotoc County Agriplex.
PHOTO BY PATTI BINGER

Larry and Blake horsing around while Blake waits to be interviewed for a job at Opryland.

Singing at a benefit in Ada, Oklahoma, not long before his move to Nashville.
PHOTO BY DIANA MASON ROSS

Rare shot of Blake during a parade in Ada honoring Ken Lance, early supporter of country music in the area.

Taking stage outdoors at the Ken Lance Tribute in Stonewall, Oklahoma.

Photo taken during the trip to find Blake a place to live in Nashville.

Two weeks out of high school, Blake made the move to Nashville. As the wide smile indicates, he was happy to be there! He had big dreams for a seventeen-year-old young man.

Blake with me and Larry, celebrating his birthday at dinner on June 18, 1994.

Blake performing on the IFCO show at Fan Fair '94.

At the home of Mae Boren Axton, who treated him to fried chicken and a birthday cake to celebrate his move to Nashville.

Totally unknown at the time but already being asked to sign autographs during Fan Fair. He stood out in a crowd at 6'5" and the hat made him even more noticeable.

Proof positive that Blake Shelton is happy anywhere! He can find fun in any situation.

Auditioning musicians for an early band at SIR Nashville.

Early fan club party back in Ada, Oklahoma, with his grandmother, Sammy Byrd.

Pausing for a photo at an autograph booth during an early Fan Fair appearance.
PHOTO BY PATRICIA JOHNSON

been able to rid for over fifteen years now. So I am going to allow her to vent right here.

> *Patti: Finally! An outlet to release my long-held grievance against another up-and-coming country singer that was working his way up the ladder at the same time as Blake. Let me preface this with the promise that I don't get mad about many things. I view most things in life as little stuff to not sweat over—concentrate on the big stuff. But every once in a while, especially if someone I know is wronged, and specifically when I know they would never have provoked what was being wielded their way, I get mad. And I hold onto it forever.*
>
> *At this point, Blake had released the mega #1 hit "Austin." He followed that up with "All Over Me," which went to #18 and "Ol' Red" #14. The villain in my story had also released three songs off of his debut album, the first going to #15, the second to #8, and the third to #1. So while Blake saw a big hit out of the gate, the other artist did the opposite. As Blake's numbers fell on subsequent releases, artist #2's rose. As has been established, Blake is a supporter of people. He doesn't understand why anyone would do anything but be supportive of another artist, even someone that is in direct competition. Artist #2 was clearly not the same. Blake was leaving an event one night and while crossing the parking lot he passed artist #2. Blake spoke as he passed when artist #2 said, "Hey Blake, what happened to you?" in reference to his falling single success. Blake was baffled. When I heard the story, I was irritated. What a petty, small man this guy was. Get over yourself, I thought. But it didn't stop there. Later, I was listening to an interview with artist #2 where they were discussing his new, and first #1 single. That's when he did it! That jerk said, and I paraphrase, that he was proud of his success. He would much rather have a slow build as had happened with his releases than come out with a five-week #1, only to follow up with a #18. Are you kidding me?! So let me give you a little lesson in karma. That was his first and last #1. He's no*

longer in country music. And now, I can let this go. Hope you have
a fantastic life from here on out; I won't give your name here, but if
you read this, you know who you are. #IYCCKGY.

Well, I hope Patti feels better now. Let us continue.

Blake's dad Dick made it to Fan Fair again that year and told *Country Weekly*, "We've been coming here for years. Even when Blake was nobody, people would line up, wanting his autograph. It happened everywhere—I guess because he's tall and wears that hat!" Later, on the main stage during the Warner Bros. portion of the show, Blake sang "Austin," "Ol' Red," and "All Over Me." The crowd welcomed him with gusto!

In August, Tony Pippin proudly announced on the front page of the *Ada Evening News*, "Shelton's album goes gold." Wow!

"Ol' Red" was the third and final release from Blake's first album. Despite the fact that it only made it to #14 on the charts, "Ol' Red" became Blake's signature song. When he went into the chorus of that song, fans would raise their right arm and keep beat to the music. We went to see him at the Ryman one time and were seated in the front row balcony when he did that song. When I saw Pete Fisher sitting in the section across from me, I actually went down there and told him Blake would make a great addition to the Opry. Yes I did! I was standing and getting into the music like everybody else when Blake spotted me. He gave me a point and a big smile as he continued the song. I'm sure I looked like an idiot. The song tells the story of an inmate outwitting his captors by using a bloodhound with an ironic ending in the style of a short story by O. Henry.

Warner Bros. collaborated with Long Hollow Winery in Nashville to bottle a special promotional wine called "Blake Shelton Ol' Red" wine. On the label was printed the following:

Blake Shelton was the biggest selling new male country vocalist
of 2001—His hit single "Austin" spent five weeks at #1—Blake is a

CRS New Faces Performer—2001 R&R Breakthrough Artist of the Year—He had the most first-week album sales of any new country male artist since 1992—And now nominated for the ACM's 2002 Top New Male Vocalist!

Unfortunately, the wine didn't help win anything that year.

"Ol' Red" did create some problems for me and Patti. A radio station somewhere decided to promote a Blake show or something like that by giving away a bloodhound. Oh my! We started getting emails by the hundreds. Animal rights activists were not happy, saying that a bloodhound is a dog that you have to really want to love. They slobber and are big and not just anyone who might win a contest would make a good owner. The station had not thought this through. After being up all night and making Blake's team aware of the issue, somebody pulled the plug on the contest. Through some good interaction with those complaining, Blake actually made some new fans. We made a little lemonade there.

The video for "Ol' Red" was cool for several reasons. It was shot at the old Tennessee State Prison where *The Green Mile* had been filmed. Blake cast good friend and NASCAR celebrity Elliot Sadler as his cousin and most of his band and crew as fellow inmates, along with the true stars of the video, the Blue tick Coonhound and Ol' Red. I loved seeing Larry breaking up rocks, taking off his cap at an inmate's funeral and high-fiving Blake in the video. Bobby Braddock was convincing as Blake's Manson-like madman cellmate. Blake's hair was going through the Sasquatch period. He had let it grow out more on the sides to stop people from saying he had a mullet. (It did nothing to curtail that talk.) When there was humidity, the hair took on a personality of its own. Blake would probably have cut it off except everyone wanted him to cut it and I have often said that he is the most stubborn *young* man I've ever known. The video, directed by Peter Zavadil, debuted on CMT's live show *Most Wanted Live* and quickly went to the #1 request spot. Personally, I think it is his best video to date.

While all of this was going on, we were trying to keep the online store stocked with unique items. We usually placed a minimum order to get stuff personalized and sold it for as little as possible to still make enough to keep things going. There was a lot of little stuff. It was good when we started adding the things he sold on the road, because we didn't have to work quite as hard on stock for the online store. We still thought it was important to have things for fan club members though, things they couldn't buy on the road. Patti liked that creative part because she was good at it, and had some great ideas through the years.

Blake wasn't crazy about having his picture on things, either through the fan club or his road merchandise. We utilized the fan club logo, a little squiggly guitar that Blake had drawn and we copyrighted for its use. One of the neatest things we had was sterling silver jewelry featuring charms of that little guitar. And for a while, we had charms that represented his #1 hits. There was one shirt Patti designed that was especially cool, kind of rock-looking. We got excited when fellow singer Clay Walker purchased one online. Of course we had the usual mugs, car tag holders, even some tiny pocket knives with his signature embossed in gold on the case. It was fun.

Finally, fan club member Anna Moser Orf, who later did photography for the annual parties, took a picture at a show that Blake liked. He had said he would do a photo shirt if he had a good live shot. He purchased rights to put Anna's photograph on the merch, and it became one of his best-selling tee shirts. Fans always wanted shirts with his picture on them. After that, they did more shirts that featured his likeness.

On the road, Blake was performing songs from his first album, *Blake Shelton*: "Austin," "Every Time I Look At You" (Blake Shelton and Doug Johnson), "All Over Me," "Same Old Song" (Braddock), and "She Doesn't Know She's Got It," (John Rich, Chris Waters, Tom Shapiro); and from his upcoming album *The Dreamer*: "My Neck of the Woods" (Don Ellis, Billy Montana) and "Playboys of the Southwestern World"; in addition to three or four cover songs made famous by the Bellamy Brothers, Eddie Rabbitt, Billy Gilman (who would later show up on *The Voice*), and closing his set with Hank Williams Jr.'s "Family Tradition." Braddock had written the song by Gilman, "The Snake Song," and fans loved the humor in it. It was all about a green garden snake falling in love with a water hose.

Either following or just before a show in Bakersfield, California, there was some off time for Blake and the crew before the next gig, so they decided to check out Kern River, made popular in a song by the great Merle Haggard. Bus driver Valerie Wren called ahead and found a secluded little town with cabins available, and they headed there. Larry recalls a town square filled with what must have been almost every citizen there to welcome Blake Shelton.

They were given directions to the cabins and settled in for a couple of days. There was a grill in front of every cabin, so Blake went into town and got some steaks and potatoes for a cook out. It was a special treat for everyone. The next day, they panned for a little gold but nobody got lucky, so after a while, they decided to try river rafting. Valerie got dumped out and hit her head on a rock and some of the others got wet, but no one was badly injured. I doubt Val got any special attention once they realized she would live and probably had to put up with some teasing about her clumsiness. Think she'll ever "swim Kern River again?"

Blake's sophomore album *The Dreamer* was completed and the first single, "The Baby" (Michael White, Harley Allen), was released October 28, 2002. Peter Zavadil again directed the accompanying video, which featured pictures and video clips of a family with three children, some from Blake's own family. It was fun for viewers to see Richie, Endy, and Blake as youngsters growing up. Of course, his family didn't follow the story line even though Blake is the baby of the family; his mom, Dorothy, was and is alive and kicking.

We still weren't above calling and requesting Blake's latest song and loved to call Gerry House at WSIX. Debi remembers hearing

Larry call in a request one morning on her drive to work. Gerry was making fun of the way Larry pronounced baby. It went something like this:

Larry: I'd like to request "The Baby."

Gerry: The Baaaabeee?

Larry: Yes, Blake Shelton's "The Baby."

Gerry: The Baaaaaaabeeeeee?

Larry: Hohboy! (Oklahoma accents do stand out.)

By far the most encouraging thing that happened in 2002 was for *Blake Shelton*, his self-titled album to go gold, meaning it had sold over five hundred thousand copies. To honor this accomplishment, Warner Bros. Records presented Blake with a special gold record plaque on *Backstage at the Opry*. Blake appropriately gave most of the credit for the success of the album to producer Bobby Braddock.

At Christmas, Blake had gold records framed and he passed them out to his band and team at a dinner in Nashville. I remember two things about that evening. I tried not to cry but I did, and in my weakened state, Blake talked me into eating a buffalo burger. I don't eat much meat anyway and buffalo meat was way out of my wheel house. But he had already laughed and pointed at me for crying so I wasn't going to be a sissy about eating a burger. I haven't had one since. (Blake loves talking me into doing things that are ridiculous for me to do. For example, if I point my foot, the second toe goes into a cramp. I can't tell you how many times he has kept on at me until I point my toe. Same result every time, followed by a belly laugh from him.) The gold record was framed in old barn wood and has a plaque with our names on it. It remains one of my favorite mementos of his rise to fame and it hangs right above Larry's computer in our home office today. It is a prized possession!

CHAPTER FIVE

I LIVED IT

By January 2003, Blake's interviews were focused on "The Baby" (Harley Allen and Michael White), which had been released a couple of months earlier and was quickly making its way to the top of the charts. It was scheduled to reach stores by February 4. Craig Havighurst of *The Tennessean* asked Blake about his story songs. Blake responded, "There's a big gap out there for a song that starts with a character and ends with a punch line. You just don't hear 'em anymore." Blake believed songs that did that stood out because they gave the audience credit for being more attentive than some radio programmers assumed they were. "Do people really listen long enough to follow a story like that in a song? "Austin" is proof that they do," Blake added with pride.

When "The Baby" was delivered, it touched a lot of people. The letters came pouring into the fan club office. I still have a folder of some of them. There was one from a lady named Pam from Bristow, Oklahoma. Her daughter, Amber, was a huge Blake fan and she and her husband had tickets to see him on Valentine's Day at Cain's Ballroom in Tulsa, Oklahoma. Just as they entered the venue, her water broke and they had to rush her to the hospital. There were complications and she had to undergo immediate surgery. Pam wanted to thank Blake because, had it not been for the concert, they would have been an hour's drive from the hospital. The baby was named Blakeley Yvonne in his honor. It just hit me that the baby is now a teenager. I wonder if she is a fan now. There were lots of letters from people who had lived out the story told in that song. Nobody sings a story song better than Blake, and you can take that to the bank.

Tony Pippin, managing editor, wrote a story dated February 11, in the *Ada Evening News*, which actually began using Blake's father's own words: "Hey Tony, Blake's got the No. 1 song in the country." It was Dick Shelton calling, obviously thrilled that his son, Blake, had topped the *Billboard* charts in country once again.

Just to give a reference point to those who didn't listen to country back then, other genres' top acts in February that year included Jennifer Lopez with LL Cool J, "All I Have" (Lopez, Makeba Riddick, Curtis Richardson, Ron G), 50 Cent, "In Da Club" (50 Cent, Dr. Dre, Mike Elizondo), Dixie Chicks, "Landslide" (Stevie Nicks), 3 Doors Down, "When I'm Gone" (Brad Arnold, Matt Roberts, Todd Harrell, Chris Henderson), and Red Hot Chili Peppers, "Can't Stop" (Flea, John Frusciante, Anthony Kiedis, Chad Smith).

Blake was happy with his second album, *The Dreamer*, which included two songs he had written, and he felt like he had some momentum going when (in a *Country Weekly* interview by David Scarlett) he said, "If you don't have a goal that you're fightin' for, you're gonna end up wastin' your life away, and that's probably what I would've done." Music was his life's ambition and he was meeting and extending his goal list frequently.

Ben Scott reviewed *The Dreamer*, again produced by Braddock, saying, "Shelton's music has more layers than an onion. He forges a discernible personality . . . even more so than his first effort." Blake felt the same way about his sophomore endeavor.

Girls were starting to really take notice of Blake by the time he played the Five Flags Center in Dubuque, Iowa. Becky Sisco covered the story by interviewing Blake and then some fans. "I like Blake Shelton's eyes," said Holly Gabel. "He's got a sexy voice," Lisa Kurth added. These were women of few words who summed up what thousands were thinking.

Don McLeese touched on the other part of what makes fans like Blake in an article for *Country Music* by reporting, "Shelton's the sort of playful jokester who puts people at ease, making even new acquaintances feel like old friends. Without a trace of the prima donna [*sic*], he's a man's man among the guys and a ladies' man around the women, yet everyone agrees that there's no b.s. in Blake Shelton." McLeese went along on a hunting trip for *The Wal-Mart Great Outdoors* program on ESPN2. He was hunting for deer in the Iowa backwoods. Producer Rich Larson found humor in how eager Blake was to shoot a deer that day. He had made a bet with fellow hunter Jack Youngblood, series cohost, of $100 for the biggest deer. Blake won the bet with an eleven-point buck. "This is the greatest day of my life," announced Blake. By the way, Blake loves the sport of hunting, but the meat does not go to waste. If he doesn't freeze it for use himself, he donates it to a food pantry somewhere.

Blake was often showing up on television. He traveled to Vancouver in April and made an appearance on Showtime's *Chris Isaak Show*. It featured several of Blake's songs that he and musician Isaak sang together. And he was cast as a designer in a CMT show decorating a room in the home that would be given away to a lucky fan. Also, he showed up in *CMT Got Me in With the Band*, which was filmed in Plymouth, Massachusetts. A fan named Jennie Cloutier won the contest and had a wonderful time hanging out backstage. She even helped Larry sell a little merchandise that day. I still follow Jennie on Facebook. I think she won the contest by agreeing to wash her hair with catsup and eggs or some such concoction. Blake also made an appearance on *The Wayne Brady Show* and the NBC drama, *American Dreams*.

My favorite television performance from the early days was one that I don't remember enough about. I am 99 percent sure that Storme Warren was the host, and I don't know why but they started running through the studio and out the door, jumping hedges, falling down, being twelve-year-old kids, and it was just fun to watch. They are the same age, but that day they were having kid fun.

"Heavy Liftin'" (Rivers Rutherford, George Teren, Boyd Houston Robert) was released April 26, followed by a video. Blake's sister Endy made her debut into acting, being cast as a dancer. She had to headbang to the song for ten hours and couldn't turn her head for two days, but it was an experience she will never forget. The song peaked at #32 and was somewhat of a disappointment. It was a little out of character for a country song, especially the video. I always thought—still do—that it would be a great theme song for a show on HGTV.

The annual fan club party that year took place at the Wildhorse Saloon in Nashville on June 4. Fans received an autographed 8×10 black and white picture of Blake that had been taken at the CMT Flameworthy Awards earlier. Everyone got an official candy bar, The BS Bar. It had a cool label featuring the Wildhorse logo, the fan club logo, and the words "I Like It Alawt." Blake had taken to using the "I like it alawt" phrase often. (I even have an email from Braddock where he used it, Blake rubbing off on him.) On the back, ingredients were listed which were actually the songs from his first two albums along with a warning, "Contents to be consumed by BS'ers only—May cause elevated levels of Blake-itis." Additional notes credit Scott and Lori Quackenbush as having manufactured the cover for the fan club. Just FYI, inside was a delicious Hershey bar. As merchandise and gifts go, we were learning that the cornier they were, the more his fans seemed to love them. I think they saw it as a way to poke a little fun back at Blake.

We were happy Blake showed up at all that year because he didn't hang around that long during the week of Fan Fair, not when he was given the pleasure of playing the annual PortFest celebration at Jacksonport State Park in northeastern Arkansas on June 6, with Earl Thomas Conley!

"Playboys of the Southwestern World" (Neal Coty and Randy VanWarmer) was released in July and only made it to #24 on the charts. It was during a time when they were questioning the importance of an expensive video and what role it had on a song's rise up the charts. There wasn't one made for this song and had they done it, it would have been a funny one no doubt. Sadly, one of the song's writers had been diagnosed with leukemia, which would take his life in about six months. I remember that Christmas, Patti designed a tree ornament that featured this song and Randy's wife, Suzi VanWarmer, ordered one.

One of my favorite fan club member stories began on August 3, 2003. Blake's Birthday Girls, Kelli Sampsel, Korrin Henkle, and Mary Beth Urton, went to an ETC concert. Larry had worked it out for them to meet Earl's guitarist and friend, cowriter of "All Over Me," Mike Pyle. The girls begged him to go get Earl because they had something for him to sign. Earl came out and the girls relayed the story Blake had told at the fan club party about going to write with him and being so nervous that the first thing he did was ask to use the restroom, and that they had brought a toilet lid for him to sign for Blake. Earl thought the whole thing was hilarious and typical Blake so he autographed it to him, "You are full of it but I love you anyway" and signed his name. Priceless! The girls took it home and had it framed to give to Blake the next time they saw him. The last time I saw it, he had it hanging in his bathroom at the first lodge he bought in Tishomingo, Oklahoma.

Fan club mail was often sweet, sharing how a song had touched a life, but there were also a few unusual requests. The most elaborate one was from a woman who claimed she and her son were disabled but she wanted to move to Nashville and had found a home for a million dollars. She thought she would be able to decorate it for an additional million. Would he send her the money? Suffice to say that Blake's home at that time was nowhere near a million dollars so he couldn't have helped with her request even if he had found it reasonable. Other favorites included the ones asking for false teeth. I was surprised the first time and amazed when it happened more than once. I have to say that I did feel sorry for anyone who needed teeth and had I myself had the money, I possibly would have helped—back then. Now, I realize that you never know when strangers are sincere. It is highly possible that by asking for a relatively small amount of money, at least compared to a two million dollar home, and coupling that with a need that would tug at heartstrings, that it was a scam request. That is probably why most people who do have money to donate give to organizations that can help a whole group of people, rather than focusing on a few. Still, I think it would be lovely to be able to help people out when you know it truly would. I have thought many times of a couple sitting across from me in a waiting room at my doctor's office. They were whispering to each other, wondering how they were going to make their house payment that month. I could tell they were hard workers and I would have loved to anonymously given them enough money to solve their problems. They were an older couple and I still think of that moment in time often.

Meanwhile, Blake went out on tour with Toby Keith's Shock'n Y'all tour, which covered thirteen states, some more than once. Larry was still merchandise manager at that time and I was teaching at Hillsboro Elementary/Middle School in Leiper's Fork, Tennessee. In August, just before school started, I went out with them on a three-day run to St. Louis, Chicago, and Kansas City. I have always tried to catch a few shows on each tour, and there is something I do each time that began with that tour. I go to a sound check and position myself in the middle of the venue. I look around and imagine that in a few hours all those seats will be occupied by fans. Then I look at Blake there on the stage, usually horsing around a little between mic tests, singing songs that never make it to the shows. Finally, I basically do the same thing that night. But for the show, I close my eyes and imagine him, the preteen at the Music Palace in Ada, Oklahoma, a chubby little boy in glasses, and I am blown away. I never fail to tear up a little when I realize how far he has come. (Actually, I just teared up a little when I reread this.) Each time, he has gone a little further. I don't know how far this young man will go with his career, but it has definitely been a slow uphill battle and I'm not sure he knows how proud we are of him and the fact that, with all the fame and fortune he has had, he is still, in my mind, the same little boy he has always been.

I realize I am repeating myself when I say that something crazy always happens when Blake is around, but that weekend during the St. Louis–Kansas City run was no exception. It was a beautiful day and I was sitting in the front of the bus watching people mill around the back of the venue. Toby liked to play basketball and had asked Blake earlier if he wanted to play, too. Blake had agreed and Toby sent someone to tell him he was ready, so I let him know. Blake, who was not even close to the same athlete Toby was, came out wearing a sweatshirt with the sleeves pushed up and a pair of Katt's terry cloth pink and white striped shorts. He had them pulled up as high as he could get them, with his buttcheeks hanging out, and was wearing a pair of tennis shoes with knee-high white socks. I grabbed a camera and as he walked around the front of the bus and waved his hand for me to put the camera down—click! Perfect! He went on out and Toby, who hadn't got out of his bus yet, could see him through the window. He sent someone out to basically "tell that boy to get dressed if he's gonna play basketball with me." I paraphrase but that was about it. Blake changed clothes and the game continued. When Blake knows he isn't great at something he always injects humor, and when he got back on the bus he was cracking up, laughing as hard as I've ever seen. All great comedians will do anything for a laugh and he fits the bill.

In September, Laverne Stewart of *The Daily Gleaner*, a daily newspaper in Fredericton, New Brunswick, Canada, printed a full-page story on Blake Shelton and his biggest Canadian fans, the Brown Family: Mary (mother), Dana (father), and five children ranging from 7–14—Allison, Christopher, Karen, Melanie, and Michael. They traveled hours south of the border in a van with no air conditioning to see Blake at shows that stretched their budget. Blake was quoted as saying, "The thing that sticks out in my mind about the Browns is that they always travel together to the shows. It's rare that you see an entire family travel together like that a long way to see a show and to say hi afterwards. That starts to stick out in your mind when you start to see them several times." The Browns were hardcore fans and I still keep up with them on Facebook. The children are all grown now and doing well.

The year wound down with the fan club newsletter celebrating its tenth anniversary. It was growing too, from a one-page publication, front and back, black and white to a four-page heavier slick paper in full color. The fan club parties went from none to Aldridge Hotel in Ada, to Douglas Corner, the Hard Rock Café, Wildhorse Saloon, and would go to Graham Central Station, and finally back to the Wildhorse Saloon in Nashville before they came to an end. The website was growing in popularity and fans were multiplying, even getting a few sign-ups from other countries. We (by *we*, I mean Patti) had started designing fan club merchandise and having loads of fun keeping Blake's fans interested. The Blake Shelton Fan Club booth in the exhibit hall at the CMA Festival had gone from one space to three and the lines were getting so long that we had to start thinking of solutions to keep everyone happy.

Blake was on the road with his first two number ones, "Austin" and "The Baby" being recognizable when he and Katt married in a private ceremony. She quit teaching and went out on the road with him for a while.

What a year 2003 had been, and it was only fitting that it had a great finale. Toby Keith, Willie Nelson, and Blake played a big New Year's Eve concert at the Gaylord Entertainment Center in Nashville. We were happy to be there and witness such a fabulous show. I do remember country music parody singer Cletus T. Judd being backstage and learning that he and Patti were born on the exact same day. Yes, it made me feel old.

Since that was Larry's last full year on the road, I asked him to go through his calendar and count the number of shows Blake had that year. With 138 shows, he was a hard working guy! Larry too! He still brags that he set up the merchandise booth early and stayed with it throughout the show, and that some of those afternoon fair shows were so hot that his tennis shoe soles melted.

Blake made a big impact in 2004 on people who attended the Country Radio Seminar (CRS) that year. (The previous year, at that same event, a bunch of industry people were hanging out at the Bridge Bar in the Renaissance Nashville Hotel, when they noticed a shadow on the ceiling reflecting a guy in his room above watching sports and enjoying his own company, if you know what I mean.) Blake decided to parody that event on video through a series of suggestive actions and music, ending up in the room appearing to be doing the same thing, but in fact, when he turned around, he was innocently strumming his guitar. He walked to the window and saw the people below laughing and pointing and had the best expression of shock on his face you can imagine. Blake later commented, "From that video on, people at least paid attention to me whenever I had a project coming up just to see what in the hell I was going to do next." He admitted it could have been a disaster, with the possibility out there that he would offend somebody, but he thought it worked in his favor in this case.

"When Somebody Knows You That Well" (Jimmy Melton and Harley Allen) had been the first release from *Blake Shelton's Barn and Grill*, and it only made it to #37, the lowest charting single of his career, so his third studio album was off to a rocky start. But that would begin to change in April when "Some Beach" (Rory Lee Feek and Paul Overstreet) was released.

As it was taking off on radio, it was decided that a video was needed. It featured many of the same friends that were spotlighted in "Ol' Red." Director Peter Zavadil filmed a guy (Blake) having a really bad day. First, he was cut off by a car driven by NASCAR's Elliot Sadler, and then had a customer (Katt) cut in front of him in the dentist's office, and finally, a nurse (Lauren Braddock Havey) called him back for his appointment, which culminated with dentist (Bobby Braddock) drilling his tooth before he was numb. The "Some Beach" video was a hoot. It soon prompted release of a video collection also titled *Blake Shelton's Barn and Grill*, which included five videos: "Some Beach"; "Austin"; "Heavy Liftin'," featuring

Endy; "The Baby," displaying old childhood pictures of Blake and his siblings; and "Ol' Red," spotlighting his road crew. Each video except "Austin" included people close to him and thus had a special connection to Blake. He has never strayed far from his family and friends. He has worked hard at staying grounded and it has only added to his success in life. "Some Beach" made its way up the charts and became a summer hit, going #1 by July and lingering on the charts an impressive four weeks. It also made it into the US *Billboard* Hot 100 at #28, no small feat for a country song.

In an April issue of *Country Weekly*, Blake shared a bring-you-back-to-reality road story with David Scarlett. He was playing a show at the Pyramid Arena in Memphis as part of Toby Keith's wildly successful Shock'n Y'all tour, and was headed backstage to eat. He was with the rest of his band and was the only one without an all-access credential when a young security staffer stopped him and asked to see his pass. Blake grinned and said, "I don't have one—if I had one, the picture on it would look . . . just like me." Everyone got a chuckle and the guard finally relented so Blake could enjoy some famous Memphis barbecue. At the very end of the article, as he was talking about how great Toby Keith was as an artist, Blake made these comments: "I don't think I'll ever be Entertainer of the Year. I'll never be that artist, like Toby is. I don't know if I have it in me. But the one thing I do know I have in me is passion for great songs. That's the one thing I know that I can do. I can bring the people a song that'll make 'em laugh or make 'em cry. And I'm happy with that."

May was a busy month for me and Larry. We had both decided to retire, me from teaching and Larry from the road. We put our home in Franklin up for sale on May 17 and it sold the next day. We didn't actually close and move until July 28, so we were still in Tennessee for the remainder of my school year and for Fan Fair.

May 30, 2004, was Larry's official last day on the road as merchandise manager, but he had fulfilled his dream and would have a pocketful of stories to tell friends at JD's, his local coffee hangout in Ada. That night, at a show in Palm Springs, California, Blake called Larry up on stage for one last performance of the rock 'n' roll medley he had done so many times at Ken Lance Sports Arena. It contained snippets of songs from his teenage years, from my least favorite, Leo Dorsey's "Ya Ya" (Dorsey, Clarence Lewis, Morgan Robinson, Morris Levy),—because Larry always sang it, "sittin' on my ya ya waitin' on my la la" instead of "sittin' here la la waiting for my ya ya" as written—to my favorite, Fats Domino's "Kansas City" (Jerry Leiber, Mike Stoller), and many others. It was bittersweet for both Blake and Larry, although neither would admit it. Time flies! A couple of Patti's classmates originally from Ada, Shawn Stevenson and Max Ross, were in the audience and one was able to snap a picture for him to commemorate the special moment.

Plans were being finalized for the fan club party, another breakfast at the Wildhorse in downtown Nashville during the Country Music Association's festival. Blake's parties were always exciting as they came close to his birthday and fans were able to celebrate that as well.

Gifts through the years were fun, starting out very personal and turning to charity donations later on as Blake requested. We put our hearts into the annual event and Blake and his fans appreciated it. That particular year, a group of members from Alberta, Canada, Darlene Gaudette, Janie Murray, and Mona Black attended thirty parties. They agreed that our party was the best and most organized of them all. You just don't forget compliments like that!

In 2004, the trusty Birthday Girls, the fan club as a whole, and members individually all chipped in on a special gift. First, the girls brought out a guitar case and when Blake opened it, he found it full to the brim with his favorite Extra sugar free gum. He would have been happy with that, but then they brought out the real gift, a custom-made Takamine guitar with his name subtly embedded between the frets in the neck of the guitar. He loved it! Of course he sat down and played a few songs for the partygoers. The first song was his signature "Ol' Red."

The website and parties were great for fans but what put the cherry on top was Blake himself. He never, ever, ever was anything other than nice, funny, witty, interested, happy, patient—I could go on and on. That is the *main* reason that the fans love him. First, his songs were great and he sounded as good live as on record and he was always responsive to them, never brushing them away or ignoring them. Talented and approachable summed up Blake's demeanor at our parties.

Once, backstage at a show, a fan grabbed his hat from his head. The teacher/mom in me came out and I was ready to reprimand her but before I could say a word, Blake reacted with something like "I need my hat back but I'll have someone try to find you a cap." Most fans were more respectful than that. Occasionally there are those who think that because they buy the music, the artist owes them something extra. Blake always gives something extra when he has a chance, but that is what it is, something extra, a gift—not something he owes.

Maybe the fan thought that because Wrangler hats issued some special Blake Shelton hats, he had plenty of them. I really don't think she was that much a thinker though. However, as part of Blake's endorsement deal with Wrangler, members of his crew got complimentary jeans and shirts. Larry wore his for years after he left the road. Wranglers last forever. In fact, he might still be wearing them but he lost a little weight and was delighted to buy a smaller size.

Anxious for the release of the album in October 2004, Blake did a commercial to promote *Blake Shelton's Barn and Grill* and it was as you might expect, hilarious. It started off with him sitting at a bar and obviously flirting with whoever was seated next to him. He used a great pick-up line; "You must be tired, you've been runnin' through my mind all night." The camera panned to the object of his affection, and it was a *sheep*! It was his idea to do a commercial with "just stupid stuff, like hittin' on a sheep in a bar, eating chicken in front of a chicken, stuff like that." The album was a fun one and he asked that the promotion embrace it as that.

Everyone loved it when *Blake Shelton's Barn and Grill* video collection went gold, and later the CD as well. Accomplishments kept coming for Blake. And, on June 13, following a performance at Country Fever in Pryor, Oklahoma, representatives from the Oklahoma Music Hall of Fame presented him with the Rising Star award. OMHF chairman Andrea Chancellor said, "Blake's escalating career made him a clear choice for our rising star award . . . We wish him the best and are so proud that yet another Oklahoman has left his mark on the nationwide music scene."

Although we had moved back to Oklahoma after our retirement in Tennessee, the fan club continued with just a different address and I had more time to devote to the club. Had it not been for my daughter Patti, who did so much in those earlier years, I would not have been able to do all we did. It was difficult enough with a full-time job. Without help from her and my daughter Debi, who helped with newsletters, it would have been impossible. Debi and I both had day jobs and Patti did not, but she made the fan club a full-time job nonetheless. It was Patti who stayed on that computer for hours every day running the website, designing fan club merchandise, and talking to fans. Our message board was a hot spot for fans back in the day.

The Hickman County, Tennessee, Ag Pavilion at Grinder's Switch Garden of Fame added a new plaque, "Blake." The dedication recognized Blake's support of Hickman County. True country music fans will recognize the name Grinder's Switch from the stories Minnie Pearl used to tell. Like Minnie, Blake had a home in Hickman County.

There was a lot going on, but when we discovered Blake ringtones were available, we couldn't wait. We have never tired of them and still use them today. Every time I get a phone call, I hear an excerpt of "Ol' Red." Patti's first one welcomed a call with Blake yelling, "Pick up the damn phone!" Unfortunately, when she was called for possible jury duty, she forgot to turn off her phone but was only slightly embarrassed. When something like that happens to any of us, we just refer to it as another funny memory, because that is what it quickly becomes. That was no exception.

In what I believe was a twist of good fortune, Blake had happened to catch Conway Twitty on an old television show singing "Goodbye Time" (James Dean Hicks and Roger Murrah) and loved it. He noticed how Twitty bent his legs and got into the song so much that he was actually sweaty. He put 100 percent into all of his performances, making him one of the most emotional singers ever in country music. Twitty had some success with that song in 1988 and Blake thought it could have a second life, so he had recorded it for the current album. Released in January 2005, it entered the top 10 and became another crowd favorite. The song, which happens to be Larry's favorite of all Blake's songs, is gripping. Bobby Braddock played it for Conway's widow Dee Twitty, and she too thought Blake's version was great.

On January 27, Blake joined Rascal Flatts' Here's to You tour. "Some Beach" had become his third #1 hit and "Goodbye Time" was the new single. Without much to do in Ada, Oklahoma, we were ready to go out for a few days with Blake on the road. The RF guys had a great show. They had a cherry picker–type machine that lifted them up and carried them above and over the entire crowd. They were a little trendier in their music and clothing than the more traditional style of Blake. They wore jeans with fancy pockets and Blake still wore Wranglers. By featuring Blake as their opening act, their show offered something for everyone.

It was during the Here's to You tour that Blake met future manager Brandon Blackstock. Brandon was the tour manager for Rascal Flatts at that time and had heard that Blake was looking for a management change. (In 2010, Blake recalled the first time Brandon brought up the subject in an interview with Donna Hughes for *The Boot*.) Blake said he would never in his life forget the incident because Brandon was Narvel's son and Reba's stepson. Blake explained, "The way it works on the Rascal Flatts tour that I found out is, they get out there and they're running around crazy and they do their show and 'good night.' They go back behind the stage, and they have to pee by then. Well, there's no time to go all the way to the bathroom because they have an encore to do. So, there's milk jugs back there with holes cut out of the top—and I don't care if they get mad at me for this—but they have to go. So, they pee in these milk jugs, right? Part of that tour was that I came out during the encore and sang the last song with them. So, they had already come out, did their show, came back, peed in the jugs and went back out and started the encore, and I'm just standing back there and Brandon Blackstock's standing right there and walks up to me and he says—and it's real loud—he says, 'Hey! I heard you're looking for a new manager, and I want you to think about me,' as he was holding two milk jugs full of urine in both hands. I remember going, 'What an idiot! What are you talking about?' But the guy was very persistent . . . I finally just decided that kind of passion is what I need in my career is a guy like that, and a guy with the power of a Narvel Blackstock and the power of a Reba McEntire."

It was also on that tour we joined Blake for lunch in catering one day and sat at a big round table with a lot of the other guys on the road. That's where I met Joe Don Rooney, the lead guitarist and high harmony vocalist from the group, and learned that he was also raised in Oklahoma. He was a very nice guy (most Okies are) and I think a brother or someone from his family was with him that day and enjoying the experience along with us. He was the same age as Blake and they all had a great time on the tour.

We all know that Blake will never completely grow up, and we actually hope not. He still sticks his finger in my nose or ear at every opportunity. He still likes to sit and listen to Larry tell stories. And, most of all, he loves to get an argument going between me and Larry. We are usually in the middle of it when I see him grinning and realize that he did it again. Strangely, most of our family feels the same way. I know my niece Mandy loves that about us; just call us Oklahoma's version of The Bickersons.

After that, Blake continued to tour pretty heavily the rest of the year. With three albums and three #1 hits, he had more of his own material to bring to the table and he was pleased about that. He still performed many cover tunes as well. Since the beginning of his touring career, he had several favorites whose songs he enjoyed singing: Conway Twitty, Jerry Reed, Travis Tritt, Eddie Rabbit, Hank Williams Jr., George Jones, the Bellamy Brothers, John Anderson, Willie Nelson, George Strait. And, all weren't country artists; you could also enjoy his take on the music of Van Morrison's "Brown Eyed Girl," Bobby Brown's "My Prerogative" (Brown, Teddy Riley, Gene Griffin), the J. Geils Band's "Centerfold" (Seth Justman), Rupert Holmes's "Escape" (The Pina Colada Song), Wild Cherry's "Play That Funky Music" (Rob Parissi), Tom Petty's "I Won't Back Down" (Petty, Jeff Lynne)—all likely inspired by his brother Richie— and later even *The Voice* costar CeeLo Green's "Forget You" (Green, Bruno Mars, the Smeezingtons, Brody Brown).

In 2005, Blake invited his mother Dorothy to accompany him to the filming of the video for "Goodbye Time" and she had a great experience. It was directed by Peter Zavadil and filmed in Marfa, Texas, a town literally in the middle of nowhere. Several movies had been filmed there, including *Giant*, which starred James Dean, Elizabeth Taylor, and Rock Hudson. Blake set it up for Dorothy to stay in James Dean's room. They actually filmed at an old farmhouse another thirty minutes out, all day for two days. She said Blake sang the song dozens of times at two or three different locations. It was supposed to look warm but was really cold. She worried about the actress who had to wear summery clothes and freeze to death. Dorothy constantly says she is forgetful, but I bet she never forgets that video shoot.

The fan club party in 2005 might have been the best one of all. Larry's sister, Linda McGaha, went along to help with the exhibit hall and party for a few years and I was glad this was one of them. It was another breakfast at the Wildhorse. The party was getting so popular that we had to limit it to members only. We always gave gifts to Blake's fans upon entry into the party. That year, they received an autographed picture and a nice glass featuring the party logo and filled with peanuts. They also got a pen imprinted with "BSers . . . Knee Deep in the Music." We had started using "BSers" long ago. At first, some of the label people weren't so sure about it but finally embraced it as, when you get to know Blake, it is *perfect!* The gift for Blake that year was two miniature donkeys, Sparkplug and Outlaw. We had to give Blake a box of toys and food for them as a way of presenting the gift because the health department wouldn't let us bring them into the venue. When Blake opened the huge box and saw two giant rubber balls, toys for the donkeys, you can imagine the comments he made. We did have a video of the two cute little donkeys, and his sound guy, Pig Parsons, showed it on the big screen. Blake sat down and sang a couple of songs with his guitar from the previous year, reminding all of us that the Takamine didn't have to be fed. See—BS—perfect!

"Nobody But Me" (Shawn Camp and Philip White), the fourth and final single from *Blake Shelton's Barn and Grill,* was released toward the end of August 2005, and would peak in mid-April 2006, at #4. Zavadil had chosen Maine as the setting for the video and fans flipped out over how handsome Blake was in those shots. He also got the opportunity to sing "Nobody But Me" in a CBS movie called *The Christmas Blessing* starring Neil Patrick Harris and Rob Lowe, which aired on December 18. Longtime fans were chomping at the bit for more Blake on television. Those who knew him recognized early that he was funny and charismatic. I always knew that he would be a talk show favorite once he was given the opportunity.

Throughout part of the year, Blake was also headlining his own Barn and Grill tour with almost fifty dates. We met up with him in August and were all in a trailer while Blake was getting his inaugural haircut from long to short before one of his first national appearances, on *Good Morning America*. We had all quit bugging him about what he called his Sasquatch hair and he had tired of it, saying it was too dang hot. Everyone was laughing and having a good time as the hair hit the floor (I even picked up some to save), but Katt made a comment, and I paraphrase, that "he isn't being himself; he doesn't act like this when y'all aren't here."

I knew then and there that it was nearing an end.

CHAPTER SIX

TIME FOR ME
TO COME HOME

B lake again joined the Rascal Flatts' guys for their Me and My Gang tour throughout the twenty-plus dates in February and March 2006. Keith Anderson and Jason Aldean also joined the group, alternating as the other opening act. At the end of the tour, Gary LeVox, Jay DeMarcus, and Joe Don Rooney presented Blake with a great gift, a classically restored 1976 (the year Blake was born) red Land Cruiser that also featured an *Ol' Red* license plate and *BS* embroidered seats. Blake was speechless. In addition, they helped him log the memory of that final show with a couple of practical jokes.

First, just as he started his performance, a black curtain dropped down in front of him, leaving the audience blocked from his view. Soon the curtain rose again and, before he continued, he filled the concertgoers in on the prank, letting them know that it wasn't a malfunction and fully realizing that it would not likely end there. The next distraction featured the local high school marching band making their way down the aisles like it was halftime at a football game. Then, a janitor came out to sweep the stage as Blake forged on with his set. Finally, while Blake wrapped it up with "Ol' Red," a man in a dog suit came out and harassed him and the band, hugging and kissing them throughout the song.

Pranks are the norm with entertainers on the road. One time, there was such an odor on the bus that all the guys were complaining. The driver, Valerie Wren, couldn't locate the smell until finally she looked under the table. Brad Paisley had removed the good stuff from a deodorized stick up, replaced it with chicken or hamburger, and stuck it under the table. As it rotted, the smell continued to get

107

worse. Not to be outdone, someone talked Val into putting some squid in the air conditioner vents atop Brad's bus. I heard the odor was so overwhelmingly nauseating that some of his group actually got sick. (Keep in mind that Larry told me this story.)

Always looking for something to pass the time between shows, Blake's mind worked in mysterious ways. Earlier, he had gone to a tattoo parlor and designed his own ink rendering of deer tracks as his personalized and unique permanent creation. Unfortunately, the final result looked very much like a line of ladybugs wrapped around his forearm. Fans had teased him relentlessly about the ladybugs. We encouraged it by having some stick-on tattoos made for them, so that form of *bugging* Blake continued for a while. This would be the year he decided to add the barbed wire around the deer tracks in a futile effort to man up the tattoo. Nice try.

Life is never a series of just music and funny stuff, even for Blake Shelton. Serious things popped up from time to time too. Oklahoma was drier than it had been during the Dustbowl days of the 1930s, which had been popularized by the John Steinbeck novel, *The Grapes of Wrath*. But in 2006, Oklahoma had been ravaged by over twenty-seven hundred wildfires. With much of the state having been declared federal disaster areas, Blake wanted to help the victims. He set up a three-day event to raise money. He called it Raindance and hosted an archery tournament, a team roping event, a silent auction, and finally a live concert in Ada, Oklahoma, on May 18, featuring himself and friends Andy Griggs, Tracy Byrd, and Keith Anderson. Over $130,000 was raised to benefit those who were devastated by the wildfires. He presented the check to Governor Brad Henry. This was Blake's first venture into fundraising for good causes, particularly in Oklahoma, but it would not be his last.

With the fan club party coming up and Blake hitting the milestone thirtieth birthday, fan club members started thinking about a gift. Blake had shared with me earlier that he hated for them to spend their money on a gift for him and would prefer they make a donation to a charity of their choice. After careful consideration,

BSers agreed that after the two donkeys, they were fresh out of ideas anyway and they wanted to do what he wished. So that year, working hard to surpass the $3,000 goal we set for ourselves, Blake would be honored by the fan club's gift of $3,135 to the St. Jude Children's Research Hospital in his name. We continued with the breakfast party but moved the venue down the street to Graham's Central Station. We wanted a little cozier atmosphere for that special year. Patti designed black tee shirts for the occasion and those who didn't get one were encouraged to wear something black for the milestone event. He good-naturedly wore a camouflage cowboy hat with a gold crown attached designed by Kelli Sampsel (fan/Birthday Girl). The crown was adorned with the words "Happy Birthday" in multi colors, music notes, and BS circles. We had hundreds of black balloons emblazoned with "over the hill" that dropped from the ceiling as everyone sang the birthday song, led by his young fan Kayla Pendergraff. He was encircled by fans that had been coming to his party for several years and he knew most of them. Many sat on the floor right up to his feet. It was indeed a special party that year.

Through the years Blake has had several managers, including Jim Sharp, Debbie Zavitson, and John Dorris, who really is the best storyteller I have ever met. I sat on the bus and listened to his stories for hours about people like Johnny Russell, Dottie West, and others. I liked John, who had also managed John Michael Montgomery and Montgomery Gentry, but 2006 would be the year Blake signed with new and younger management at Starstruck Management Group.

Brandon Blackstock had been the tour manager for Rascal Flatts for a few years. But ten years earlier, he had started in the mailroom at Starstruck Entertainment and would be returning to work with his dad, Narvel Blackstock, to manage the career of Blake Shelton. Looking back, this was one of Blake's best moves ever, ranking up there with choosing Bobby Braddock as his first producer. His career has steadily climbed faster and higher than ever before. Brandon looks just like a younger version of Narvel, but I know Brandon much better. One night on the bus, I ran up and gave Narvel a big hug thinking he was Brandon. It embarrassed me to death and Blake thought it was hilarious. I know he was enjoying my humiliation. Later when we talked about it, Brandon just said that his dad would be happy to know he looked that young. Brandon is close to Blake's age as is Kevin Canady (tour manager), another great guy who is fantastic at what he does. Blake has surrounded himself with a good team.

Blake made another television appearance as himself in a hilarious sketch on Jeff Foxworthy's show. In it, Foxworthy went to the doctor for a routine exam but his doctor lost his fancy new phone during the examination, and they were both shocked when they discovered where it was lost. Blake arrived for his appointment and needed to borrow the phone for a radio interview. Picture Jeff Foxworthy leaning over the examination table with Blake talking and singing to his bum. People were beginning to realize that Blake is funny. Getting to see him on television was always exciting for fans as it would give them their Blake fix when he wasn't coming to their area for a concert often enough to suit them.

Oklahomans are especially happy when Blake is anywhere in the state, and that year he performed to a huge crowd at the Oklahoma State Fair. He had made a side trip to see Endy and meet his new niece, Ryan, and got stuck in traffic on the way to the fair. He told those in attendance what had happened and that only one song was going through his head, "Some Beach." It was the perfect transition into the song.

He had completed his fourth studio album, *Pure BS*, which would be released in May of 2007. Bobby Braddock had been sole producer on the previous three, but Warner Bros. wanted to bring in some new blood in the form of a couple of different producers for this project. Brent Rowan and Paul Worley shared production duties with Braddock. "Don't Make Me" (Marla Cannon-Goodman, Deanna Bryant, and Dave Berg), his first single produced by

Rowan, and a video by Roman White were released almost simultaneously in November. The song would climb to #12 before dropping from the charts.

Another opportunity to give back came when Cracker Barrel and Vector Management partnered to donate $125,000, a portion of the proceeds of a CD featuring Blake singing "The Gambler" (Don Schlitz), originally made famous by Kenny Rogers, to the Country Music Hall of Fame. Other artists covered well known hits by other performers.

Meanwhile, Blake bought a home in Ada and Katt moved back to Oklahoma while he put the farm in Centerville, Tennessee, on the market. They divorced in 2006.

Blake referred to the year he celebrated his thirtieth birthday as one of the toughest years of his life. He went through so many changes, adding a couple of new producers on the latest album, hiring new management, and going through a divorce—a lot for one year.

The home in Tennessee had sold quickly and Blake had actually been living on his bus. He decided that he was ready to move back to Oklahoma and asked everyone to keep their eyes open for a place he could enjoy. He found one possibility in Konawa, near Ada, but when the seller realized who wanted to buy it, the price went up and he lost interest. He wanted a place to live, but he was far more interested in land than a house. Patti found something online near Tishomingo that seemed perfect and there were a lot of pictures available. I forwarded them to Kevin Canady and asked him to show the property to Blake, who immediately called a realtor. It was just what he wanted. There was a lot of land and a simple lodge that had been originally built for hunters, not fancy at all. The concrete block house had a big open area for kitchen, dining, and living and a wide hall with two bedrooms separated with a bathroom on each side. He bought the twelve hudred acres with the hunting lodge and quickly made it his home. Dorothy helped him decorate it with a lot of camouflage accessories, bedspreads, towels, and the like and he hung that toilet seat autographed by Earl Thomas Conley in his bathroom. There were a lot of deer heads adorning the walls in the living area and family pictures lining the walls of the hall. He had a jukebox in the eating area. It had Blake Shelton written all over it. The floors were concrete so Blake didn't have to be concerned about tracking mud into the house. I remember one time, he was mowing and drove the lawn mower right in through the front door and straight out the back.

After the marriage ended, Blake and Miranda Lambert had started seeing each other on a regular basis. She bought an old farmhouse with seven hundred acres and a barn about six miles from Blake's large property in Tishomingo.

Blake loved Oklahoma and his new place, but he was also busy preparing for Raindance II. It took place April 21–24, 2007, in Ada and included all the events he had the previous year with the addition of a Celebrity Shoot-Out. Blake insisted ticket prices remain low, so at $30, nobody would be excluded. More sponsors jumped on board this time and again Raindance was a huge success. Neal McCoy, Steve Holy, and Craig Morgan were on hand and the event garnered well over $100,000. The fan club surprised Blake with a donation of $9,500. After the show Craig Morgan told me that what he loved most about Blake was that he was always the same guy, that he hadn't changed. He still hasn't.

Pure BS, the fourth studio album, was released in May. The second single release, "The More I Drink" (David Lee Murphy, Chris DuBois, Dave Turnbull), saw airplay in July, peaking in December at #19. At this point, Blake had three number one songs from three different albums, and scattered throughout, nine other singles with moderate success, notably "Nobody but Me" and "Goodbye Time," which had broken into the top 10.

Blake was really proud of a song he wrote with Kosser and Braddock, the final song on the album, appropriately titled "The Last Country Song." It had some lines from songs earlier recorded by George Jones and John Anderson so Braddock called them and asked if they would come in and sing those lines. They agreed and Blake was on cloud nine! It was never released as a single but was a special song for Blake in so many ways.

While he was promoting *Pure BS, Country Weekly* reporter Shane Tarleton noted that he had no curls anymore but he still wore a hat, and then asked him how he would describe his style. Blake responded, "Country." I think that would be the same answer today even without the hat.

Preparations for the *Coolest Party in Town* were underway and that included making the move back to the Wildhorse for another huge buffet breakfast. The meet and greet with Blake at the party had been changed a little. There wasn't enough time to do it all live. He personalized and pre-autographed his picture so we could hand those out at the door, along with the party gift, which that year was a red six-pack cooler with the theme of the party printed on the front in black. But everyone got to go through the line onstage and have their picture taken with Blake. And, Blake performed an acoustic set of songs concert goers did not necessarily get to hear at shows on the road. Fans were excited when Blake invited them to participate in a new video; many took him up on it. Roman White's "The More I Drink" video was filmed later that week just outside of Nashville.

Also, fan club member Donna Dunnam was inspired by Flat Stanley to adopt a stuffed bull named Buford T. Shelton and send him out on the road. Buford was introduced at the party. He went from fan to fan and city to city spreading the BS and would quickly become Blake's most traveled fan. Fan club members were allowed to make a date with Buford and he was photographed at all kinds of places and especially at Blake's shows. He also attended other country concerts and had his picture taken with other stars. His wardrobe grew with each visit and he soon had to travel in a pretty big case. He was definitely a big topic of conversation for about five years until he retired.

We caught Blake's concert in Las Vegas at The Railhead that year on July 7. His new backdrop featured huge flames with *Pure BS* emblazoned right in the center. His new show was what it always was and continues to be, better than the last one. He just keeps getting better and better.

Also, in July that year, while Blake was in Ada visiting Dorothy, his Uncle Dempsey Byrd called and said there was a strange man in his house. They raced over and Blake apprehended the intoxicated would-be burglar, who was arrested. Blake always had a special place in his heart for Dempsey. It devastated him when only two short months later, his uncle was struck and killed by a car while walking down a street in Ada, Oklahoma. He was seventy-two. Fan club members immediately wanted to do something in memory of Blake's uncle so we had a tree planted and a plaque placed at Glenwood Park near Dempsey's home in Ada.

Under new management, Blake continued to be seen periodically on television. He made an appearance on the Paula Deen cooking show. She had him make a cowboy brisket. He said that he had never made one before but "Oklahomans had been rubbing their meat for years." He was developing a penchant for the double entendre and that definitely got a laugh. Then he sang "Don't Make Me" to Paula, who portrayed the ultimate swooning fan. The show ended with a bang when she laughingly crawled into Blake's bed on his tour bus. I think he might have met his match with this woman old enough to be his mother. Showing that she could be every bit as raunchy as him, he seemed to be genuinely embarrassed. The Food Network deserved a high five for having the courage to do a show featuring those two!

He also made an appearance on the Craig Ferguson show and did a sketch during the ACM Awards show with comedian Ron White. Our biggest television news for the year was NBC casting Blake to be a celebrity choir leader on a new reality show, *Clash of the Choirs*. Daughter Debi remembers attending the auditions for the show at the old Farmers Market building in downtown Oklahoma City.

We make our big move to Franklin, just outside of Nashville in 1996. PHOTO BY LINDA MCGAHA

Megan Sheehan with Blake before performances at Libby's Steakhouse in Kentucky. PHOTO BY MEGAN SHEEHAN

Blake happy about a putt during a miniature golf game.

Taking a break in my Franklin home office after cataloging songs Blake had written.

Blake with Chickasaw Nation governor Bill Anoatubby following an event in Ada.

Blake during an online chat with fan club members during the transitional year without a party.

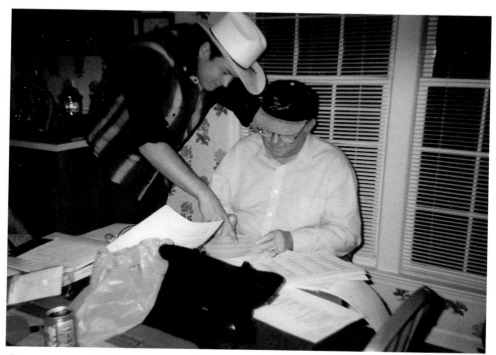

Going over a publishing contract with Larry.

Visiting with Matthew Gilliam at WSM Radio in Nashville.

Debi and Blake posing for a shot at our home in Franklin.

Blake with Michael Kosser, the man who introduced him to Bobby Braddock.

Blake with Bobby Braddock, the man who got him his record deal and produced his first albums.

My favorite picture of Blake, taken at Fan Fair right after he signed with Giant Records.

Blake in a cheesy mood, holding up a single that went out to early fan club members.

Blake with Mark Collie during intermission at Blake's Hillsboro Nights concert in Leiper's Fork, Tennessee.

The Birthday Girls (Kelli Sampsel, Mary Beth Urton Garner, and Korrin Henkle Bowers) with Blake. PHOTO BY SHERRY URTON

Blake performing his magic. PHOTO BY ANNA MOSER ORF

Blake visiting with fans.
PHOTO BY ANNA MOSER ORF

First action shot that Blake liked and approved for use on a t-shirt.
PHOTO BY ANNA MOSER ORF

Blake joked that he was no choir boy, but he loved the show. Other celebrities participating included Patti LaBelle, Kelly Rowland, Michael Bolton, and Nick Lachey. Lachey's team came in first, LaBelle second, and Blake third. His team of twenty Oklahomans received a check for $50,000 and it was split between Army Morale Welfare Recreation (MWR) and Project Rebuild. It aired in December and there was one person that Blake had to take to that show for sure, his mom. She loved Michael Bolton and Blake teased her that she called him "Michael Bolkey." I'm thinking NBC took note of how photogenic, quick-witted, and talented this newcomer was and how he held his own with the other celebrities. He had an instant rapport with Nick and referred to him as Nick *Latch-ee*. Maybe NBC would keep all this in mind in case something else came along later. You think?

Back home, Blake's state was celebrating a milestone year. The word *Oklahoma* comes from the Choctaw Indian words for Red (Okla) and People (Humma) and in 2007, Oklahoma was celebrating its centennial with a year of events and offering a two-disc set called *Oklahoma Rising* featuring Oklahoma talents Vince Gill, Jimmy Webb, Toby Keith, Reba McEntire, Carrie Underwood, Kristin Chenoweth, Garth Brooks, Joe Diffie, and Blake Shelton, among others. The grand finale was the Oklahoma Centennial Spectacular concert featuring an unprecedented number of famous Oklahoma sons and daughters. Among celebrities were Reba McEntire, Garth Brooks, Vince Gill, Carrie Underwood, Toby Keith, Blake Shelton, the Flaming Lips, Patti Page, Jimmy Webb, Johnny Bench, Bart Conner, Leona Mitchell, five Miss Americas, Willard Scott, N. Scott Momaday, Rance Howard, and Shirley Jones. It was the grand finale to a year filled with over a thousand projects and events. There are actually thirty-nine sovereign nations, Native American tribes, which operate as independent governments in Oklahoma. Ada is home to the Chickasaw Nation and Blake has worked closely with Governor Bill Anoatubby on several occasions. That night was all of Oklahoma and we were in the audience when Blake performed the Jimmy Webb classic "Wichita Lineman," made famous by Glen Campbell. Blake had made sure we had good seats to the show and we enjoyed every minute; seeing Blake amid all that incredible talent was extra special.

On the heels of the success of *Clash of the Choirs*, Blake was given his first shot at judging in 2007 as he joined fellow judges Randy Owen and Anastasia Brown on season 5 of a weekly talent show, *Nashville Star,* on the USA Network. He had the opportunity to critique in a generally positive way and offer suggestions to the talent that crossed the stage. What made it different from *American Idol* was that it featured country vocalists. The year that Blake judged, an eighteen-year-old Kacey Musgraves came in seventh, not getting a label deal with Mercury Nashville for five more years and managing to win CMA's New Vocalist of the Year award and two Grammys for her songwriting by 2013. You just have to "Follow Your Arrow" (Brandy Clark, Shane McAnally, Kacey Musgraves).

In February, *Blake Shelton: Collector's Edition*, was available exclusively at Walmart and included Blake's current hit "Home" (Michael Buble) as well as "Austin," "Ol' Red," "Nobody but Me," and "Some Beach." With the success of "Home," a reissue of *Pure BS* called *Deluxe Edition* came out in May and included "Home" and two previously unreleased songs written by Blake, "Chances" and "I Can't Walk Away." "Home" became his fourth #1 in July.

Country will always be Blake's favorite, but he has learned to appreciate all music. "Home" was so special that everyone involved had wanted to get it out there for people to hear rather than wait for the next album. So the two subsequent rereleases happened, with positive results.

Speaking of Blake's favorite music, he loves Dean Martin and had made that known somewhere along the line. Martin's daughter once sent him a huge box of all of his recordings. And he loves Christmas songs, listens to them all year. So listening to Dean Martin sing Christmas songs would make for the perfect evening. You know, despite Martin's reputation as a perennial drinker, Jerry

Lewis insisted that it was apple juice in the glass. In a touch of irony, Dean Martin died on Christmas Day in 1995.

On May 23, Blake had the honor of representing country music as a guest on the one-night-only concert David Foster and Friends: Hit Man at Mandalay Bay in Las Vegas. It was televised and followed by a CD. Blake sang "Home" with Michael Bublé, a song originally recorded by Bublé, who took it to the top of *Billboard*'s contemporary chart, followed by Blake's version going to the top of the country charts. It was actually written by Bublé along with Alan Chang and Amy Foster-Gillies (David Foster's daughter). Blake also sang "Wildflower" (Doug Edwards), which was a cover of one of Foster's favorites, made popular by Skylark. The show was highly entertaining and fans loved seeing Blake branch out, fitting right in with performers from other genres.

The VIP fan club party tickets in 2008 were gone in under ninety-six hours. Word had spread that Blake's party was the best one out there and many joined every year just to get to attend one. Patti greeted fans at the door and checked them off the list and sent them on to Patty Kerckhoff (teacher/friend) to get their gift packet, which included a personalized and autographed picture of Blake. If they ordered a party shirt, they picked that up from Warren K. (Patty's husband/friend) and moved on to David (Patti's husband/son-in-law) for their gift of a party convertible cap/visor. David wouldn't give up the gift until they gave him a smile. One fan, who was probably worn out from the week's events, gave him a half-hearted smile and he unzipped the crown of the cap and handed the visor to her saying, "Half a smile, half a cap." She quickly gave him a big grin and got the rest of her cap. From there, they went on inside the main part of the venue and met Larry who helped them find a seat and explain about the breakfast buffet. Anna Moser (fan/friend/photographer) took the pictures and the line moved so quickly that I had to give away door prizes before Blake's performance. Chances of getting one were excellent as Wrangler had given us thirty gift certificates for jeans and ten Wrangler jackets. We also gave out Shotgun Shel-tons (Wranglers that Blake had actually hung in a tree and shot up with his shotgun), *Pure BS* albums (donated by #1 fan Connie Shultz), caps, toy trucks, just lots of stuff. David came out and shot t-shirts all over the place. It was big fun!

When he came out, Blake told his diehard fans, "I'm more comfortable than I've ever been in front of y'all. So thank y'all for always being there." He explained that it was the first party that he wouldn't be playing the guitar they had given him years earlier because he accidentally left it on the bus and the bus had already headed out for the next show in California. But he sat on a stool and with just him and a guitar, sang a string of hits, ending with the signature "Ol' Red."

As a surprise, Blake gave his fans the responsibility of choos-ing his next single. Everyone sat quietly and listened as the new songs were played over the speakers. They had three to choose from and the winner was "She Wouldn't Be Gone" (Jennifer Adan, Cory Batten).

Buford T. was there with a sign that read "44,111 miles traveled spreadin' BS." The party was another success, ending with more blasts from the air gun loaned for the occasion by Citizens Bank of Ada. Larry shot more t-shirts all around, including both balconies, as he hollered, "See you next year!"

Doing things for fans like giving them the opportunity to be in a video, choosing the next single, taking the time to have a pic-ture with them, sitting down at a party and answering questions and singing songs, and even taking requests created a hardcore fan base!

That was also the year Patti and I decided to give him a crazy gift. She had seen the Hula chair on the *Ellen* show. So, as we were taking donations from members for the annual charity donation in Blake's name, Patti and I were shopping for the chair. All of the money taken in by fans went to the charity, while the crazy chair was from me. When I presented it to him at the party, I told him that I had found the solution for him to be able to kill two birds with one stone. He never really liked to exercise and this chair rotated and twisted all over the place giving him a workout, and while he was in the chair he could make his morning radio calls. I suggested he take it for a ride. I asked him to get in the chair and call his mother, who didn't make it to the party that particular year, so he could talk while the chair exercised him to see what it would be like. He was literally twisting that 6'5" frame all over the place, and when Dorothy asked him what he was doing, he said that he was "on stage at his fan club party being molested by a chair." You can watch that memorable moment on YouTube by searching "Blake Shelton Fan Club 2008." We also presented him with a check for $10,605 made out to his favorite charity, which at the time was Oklahoma-based and helped people rebuild homes destroyed by fires.

I think this was my favorite of all the parties, and I loved them all! (OK, they were all my favorite.) The media covered this one well. *Country Weekly, People* magazine, *CMT, GAC, The Tennessean,* and others were there in full force.

Always looking for ways to make fans laugh, Blake had started writing cheesy poems that he would recite during his concerts, adapting the poetry to fit the city. Google "Blake Shelton poems" to find a few on YouTube and get the full effect of the humor. He recited one of those poems at a show in Atchison, Kansas, on July 18, 2008. His recitation made it obvious that he realized it was of course, pure silliness, and the audience was in on the joke, making comments back to him and laughing at the end of each line. Due to all the interaction, it took him four minutes to recite the short poem.

He began by saying, "This poem I wrote is to explain to y'all who I am, and it's called 'What It's Like to be Blake Shelton' (long pause) by Blake Shelton."

1976 was the year I was born just a little bit south of here.
Mom cried when she saw my face; Dad was out drinkin' beer.
Growin' up in Oklahoma, a kid can get bored;
there isn't that much to do.
I once got in trouble for hittin' a kid in the head—with dog poo.
Major tours and county fairs, lookin' back at where I've been,
I've learned how to put on a pretty good show and sing out while
suckin' in.
I've picked with Hank, I've picked
with George Jones, I've picked with
ETC.
I picked up a girl in Kansas one night
and now it burns when I pee.

He stopped, turned around like he didn't remember writing that
part and said, "Who wrote that—I think Trent put that in there."

I've acted a bit, I've led a choir; hell, I've even sang a few jingles.
Sometimes I miss home, I wanna go home—
just promotin' my new single.
As for my hobbies, well that'll never change,
I shoot deer and catch bass.
Oh, and if you don't think I oughta' be shootin' deer . . .
well, you can kiss my ass.
I'm 32 years old now, my girl is 24; some say she's way too young,
But I've stuck with her, is it love or fear?
She's pretty damn good with a gun.
In closing I'll say that life's been great,
and I love what I do, I swear.
I thank you the fans and God up in heaven . . .
that I wasn't born with Craig Morgan's hair.

Blake made an appearance on the *Today* show in August to
talk about "Home," which had gone #1 in July, and being named

one of *People* magazine's Hottest Bachelors. Meanwhile, *Country Weekly* named him one of Country's Top 10 Sexiest Men. He was starting to show up more and more on television. "She Wouldn't Be Gone" hit radio airwaves in August, followed by a Scott Speer video later in the year. It continued to climb the charts for the remainder of the year.

In October, Blake had a show in Primm, Nevada, so we decided to fly to Las Vegas and meet up with friends Patty and Warren, catch the show, spend a few days at the Grand Canyon, and go back to Vegas for a show or two before flying home. It was always fun to sit around with Blake and old friends talking about the early days in Nashville. One of the memories we relived was the time we had rented some cabins outside Nashville just to be together and do some boating. I don't know how it happened because Warren isn't a big guy, but he had sat on a concrete bench and it cracked right in the middle dumping him unceremoniously onto the ground. It prompted one of Blake's big belly laughs.

He had quit doing the big belly laughs as much because they had created some vocal problems. When we were still in Nashville, he had developed nodules on his throat and I insisted he go to a doctor. I did a little research and took him to one that Reba had used and we took him in to have them checked. The doctor removed them and I guess it was a pretty painful experience because he said he would never do that again! He may have even been a little angry with me for pushing it.

The new album, *Startin' Fires,* was released in November and its first single, "She Wouldn't Be Gone," was continuing its climb. Scott Hendricks entered the picture as the producer on all but two songs. Braddock and Rowan each had a song on this album but neither was released as a single. *Country Weekly* pondered why Blake wasn't winning awards—all his fans were wondering the exact same thing. What the heck?

Later that year, the fan club changed as Warner Bros. became more involved and would be taking over the fan club. There was an insert in the new album announcing a new Blake Shelton Fan Club coming soon. After fifteen years, we stopped doing the newsletter and ended with an edition to thank most of those who had helped through the years including Connie Schultz (#1 poster and voter), Scott Quackenbush (web tech), and Anna Moser (photographer). Thanks also went to Mike and Angie Stafford, who were instrumental in Blake's early career, and of course his family. From 1998, my daughter Patti Binger had been the website designer/manager and for thirteen of those years, my daughter Debi Large was editor of the newsletter. Changes are sometimes difficult, maybe even more so as you get a little older, and this hit me pretty hard. Blake was getting bigger all the time, and as he did, changes were inevitable. I had realized this day would come but I still wasn't really happy about it. Bobby Braddock had also begun sharing duties with other producers and Edyie Brooks Bryant couldn't have been happy when Wrangler was dropped as a sponsor. But I knew without a doubt that Blake still loved all of us.

Blake was busy promoting *Startin' Fires* a lot that year and took a much-needed break in December, spending two full weeks at his home in Tishomingo, Oklahoma. What do you do in Tish? *Hunt*!

CHAPTER SEVEN

HILLBILLY BONE

"I'll Just Hold On" (Ben Hayslip, Troy Olsen, Bryan Simpson) was released on February 23, 2009, and would peak at #8. It was the second and final release from *Startin' Fires*, Blake's fifth album in a row that yielded one #1 song, in this case the first release "She Wouldn't Be Gone," the song selected by fans at his party the previous year.

On February 24, 2009, at 5:00 p.m., I turned blakeshelton.com over to Blake so that Warner Bros. could control it. I had purchased it along with .net and .org when those were the three main domains and I did it for Blake. I spoke to Mary Ann McCready, his business manager, and told her that I would give it to Blake and hoped he would maintain ownership and let the label use it. I tried my best to hang onto the fan club, but Warner Bros. felt it best to take it over, and Blake seemed to agree. I would no longer be in charge of the website or the online merchandise, but they did buy out my inventory and made arrangements for some future payments. I spoke to both Narvel and Brandon and felt they handled it professionally. Patti and I helped with the transfer as much as possible once the decision was made. We did have a peaceful transition. Dana Kelley Lobb, who was executive assistant for Starstruck Management Group from 2006–2015, was always great. Berkley Myers and Alissa Endres, managers at Starstruck, continue to be helpful when I need or want something. We still helped monitor the message board for a while and were told we could keep the fan club party. We did have one for three more years before it too was eliminated. I would continue to be the fan club president, but it is really only an honorary title now. Our number one priority was always to do what was best for Blake and a change of this kind had no effect on our friendship.

Also in February, Blake and Miranda treated Johnston County, Oklahoma, where Blake now calls home, to a benefit concert. Over $70,000 was raised to expand and improve the Tishomingo Animal Shelter and to provide for the welfare of abandoned animals in the area.

And then one day out of the blue, Blake called and asked what we were doing and said to "come over to dad's house . . . I have a surprise." I grabbed my video camera and we drove the few blocks to where Dick lived. Blake surprised him with a 1957 Chevrolet, a classic. Dick was all smiles and happy as could be that day. Endy joked that Blake one-upped her for Father's Day, because it made her coffee mug look bad. You gotta love that Okie sense of humor! I know that Blake was happy to be able to give back to his parents. He later gifted his mother with ten acres near where he lived for her and husband Mike Shackleford to build a new home. Mike also built a huge shop and continued to help Blake take care of the animals and watch things for several years before he too retired. Blake and Mike had been fishing buddies for years. When Mike went out with Blake once, fans thought he was Kris Kristofferson and Blake got a big kick out of that. Mike does favor Kris.

Endy had married Mike Intrieri, who shares Blake's love of the great outdoors, and they now have two children, Ryan and Jace. I remember them dropping by at Christmas when Jace was just a baby. This may embarrass him since he is getting older, but I thought he was the most beautiful little baby I had ever seen. Along with Dick's wife Terrie, that made up Blake's family. Of course his extended family was already enormous and by this time cousins were having children, and some even having grandchildren, so they were really growing in number. Blake usually managed to get together with everyone at least once a year, normally during the holidays. I remember one time when he had a show in Oklahoma and one of his uncles was in his meet and greet line. He thought that was ridiculous because he had just seen him on Thanksgiving. I think the uncle was enjoying telling everyone in the line that he was related to Blake. With good cause, everyone was extremely proud of Blake.

Blake had called to let us know he was opening for George Strait at the grand opening of the new Dallas Cowboy Stadium on June 6, 2009, and wanted to know if we wanted to go. Yes! I don't know how it happened that we had never seen George Strait in person. We have always been huge music fans and have seen almost everyone live at some point, even before Blake was born. It was a bonus to also see Blake on the same show. We had great seats and George did not disappoint, nor did Blake. Blake joked about the people in the balconies looking like ants. He had some funny lines but I can't remember even one. The place was gigantic and the roof could be opened, which amazed me. Before the show, we were following Blake to the dressing room or rehearsal or something and he was in a golf cart with another guy. The guy hopped out to give me his seat and he sat on the hood. Later, Blake asked if I knew who that was and I did not. It was Jay Cutler, quarterback for the Chicago Bears. So, that next season, I rooted for *"da Bears"* (a little *SNL* reference there). It had been advertised that Julianne Hough would also perform, but Lee Ann Womack was there instead and she was great. It is a wonderful memory.

For the 2009 party, Blake decided to move it to a nighttime event and bring his entire band. He loved music from the 1980s and wanted to focus on that decade. Guests included Laura Bell Bundy, Hillary Scott of Lady A, Nan Kelley, and Megan Sheehan among others. We continued to have it at the Wildhorse, but Blake wanted to move it to the evening. In the past he hadn't been able to sleep the night before for fear he wouldn't wake up in time for his own party. It was much easier to plan because the meal portion of the party was eliminated. Blake invited good friend Steve Wariner to be his special guest that year. Steve sang a song and then gave Blake his guitar. Blake hugged the guitar and then Steve. His hugs are always so long that he finally makes the recipient uncomfortable enough to actually push him away.

Dan Seals had passed in March from mantle cell lymphoma and friend Nan Kelley (who Blake calls "the sweetest woman he has ever met") was in remission from Hodgkins Lymphoma, so Blake asked that we make the Leukemia and Lymphoma Society (LLS) the recipient of fan club donations from that point forward. For his birthday that year, we presented $11,400 to LLS. Blake sang the Dolly Parton/Kenny Rogers hit "Islands in the Stream" (Bee Gees) with Nan, and the fans loved it.

In September that year, we got a group together to represent Blake in Oklahoma City at the LLS Light the Night walk. That year marked the beginning of several years working with this wonderful organization, all because Blake loved Dan and Nan.

By 2009, Blake was starting a stir on Twitter with his hilarious posts. Blake has almost twenty million followers who took to *Twitter* for this:

It's gotta suck for tabloids that I personally have more followers on Twitter than they have buyers . . . Ha! Ha! #blowme #thenwriteaboutit

Just cut my finger trying to open a can of whup ass

Decided to relieve myself this morning off our 14th floor condo balcony . . . It was so scary to hang my rear that far over the edge!

Damn it! If my urine won't catch fire then why does it burn so bad when I pee?!

Ha! Ha! I'm driving and tweeting! I'm driving and twe

Call the doctor if your erection lasts more than 4 hours?! Bullshit! I'm calling the newspaper!

Dear iPhone . . . No I'm not trying to spell shut! Or shot! Or duck!! Or fudge!! You piece of shut . . . Damn it!!

Just sitting here in a tree thinking about the fact that I've gone Hollywood

Me: Hey I need to hit the restroom during the commercial break. Security: OK but you have less than 2 and a half . . . Me: You've seen it?!

Holiday Help . . . by Blake Shelton. Hate being asked to do the dishes after Christmas dinner? Drop some of Mom's fine china . . . Hello football!

And when some of his tweets hit a nerve, Blake was quick to issue a heartfelt apology like the one below:

Everyone knows comedy has been a major part of my career and it's always been out there for anyone to see. That said anyone who knows me also knows I have no tolerance for hate of any kind or form. Can my humor at times be inappropriate and immature? Yes. Hateful? Never. That said I deeply apologize to anybody who may have been offended.

Of course, the fans loved tweets like the one below offering a free popup show:

Denver Colorado . . . You! Grizzly Rose Doors at 6:00 PM First come, first serve

For a while Blake enjoyed wearing what he called Shotgun Sheltons, Wrangler jeans that had been pummeled with buckshot from a shotgun. We went down to his place in Tishomingo and he and Larry shot up a bunch of them one afternoon. Blake wore them at shows for a while and autographed many of them for auctions to raise money for LLS. I thought it was the coolest idea ever for jeans and still don't know why it didn't catch on. They had a unique look . . . guess it didn't show enough skin. I still have one pair just in case Blake ever wants to put them in a museum.

GAC sent a film crew to Ada during the filming of a *Backstory* (season 1, episode 3) on Blake. Part of it was shot at our home. It was pretty exciting to have a makeup room set up in our bathroom and people all over the place. It was finally decided to put a couple of chairs in our living room as the location for me and Larry to be interviewed. Larry always wears a cap and they wanted him to remove it. He would not have been comfortable without it and Brandon Blackstock recognized that and said something like "Leave the cap, it's Larry." We were asked questions about Blake's early days. Larry has always been better in front of a camera and did a great job. Years of performing in a country band as well as being a principal of different schools around Oklahoma and Tennessee prepared him to be able to speak far more eloquently than I ever could. I was honored to be represented as a part of it as well.

"Hillbilly Bone" (Luke Laird and Craig Wiseman), featuring Trace Adkins as a guest vocalist, was released in October and another Roman White video accompanied it. This song impacted Blake's career much like Reba McEntire's "Whoever's in New England" (Kendal Franceschi, Quentin Powers) did hers twenty years earlier, and I think for the same reason: they included references outside the South. It allowed fans in those other areas to identify with the song better.

Once again, Blake wasn't nominated for an award of any kind. Taylor Swift was the big winner at the CMAs that year and Carrie Underwood at the ACMs. Blake continued his tours and other endeavors as if to say, "I will not be ignored."

Blake performed at a Murray State College concert in Tishomingo to benefit rescue animals and shelters through the Mutt-Nation Foundation. It included a silent auction and dinner in addition to the actual concert. He was constantly doing fundraisers to benefit locals in the area and still touring heavily.

Hillbilly Bone, the album, debuted at number two on the US *Billboard* Top Country Albums chart in March under the Warner Music Group's Reprise label. It was the first one totally produced by Scott Hendricks, the first extended play album, an experiment

Blake called the Six Pack that included only six songs, making it less expensive. The first one also included "Kiss My Country Ass" (Rhett Akins, Dallas Davidson, Jon Stone), which was not released as a single but became a concert favorite. The plan was to release three what I called mini-albums a year. The only song released from this effort was the title track "Hillbilly Bone," which was #1 in the nation by March and would begin a record number of consecutive #1s. Blake's Hillbilly Bone tour promoted the album.

Scott Hendricks is another Okie. Born in Clinton, Oklahoma, he attended Oklahoma State University. (Ironically, he roomed with the dad of Blake's first real girlfriend, Ashley Stephenson.) He coproduced thirty #1 hits in the 1990s and from 2010, he has produced Blake's albums.

The title track from Blake's second extended play *All About Tonight* (Rhett Akins, Ben Hayslip, Dallas Davidson) was released in April followed by his first live video, directed by Jon Small. It was first viewed on CMT on June 16. The song of the same title reached #1 on August 28, 2010 (Larry's birthday), just weeks after the album release.

Because someone recognized that the song was perfect for a concert kick-off, Blake went to Evansville, Indiana's Roberts Municipal Stadium to film *Blake Shelton Live: It's All About Tonight*. The ninety-minute show, which featured twelve songs and behind the scenes antics, aired on the Great American Country (GAC) television channel.

I'm sure publishing companies give artists a trophy every time they have a #1 song written by one of their writers (in this case Luke Laird), but what made the one Blake received from Universal Music Publishing for *Hillbilly Bone* is that he gave it to me. How cool is that!

Blake and Trace won the CMT Music Award for Collaborative Video of the Year: "Hillbilly Bone."

In April, Blake and Trace Adkins won the Vocal Event of the Year award at the 45th Annual Academy of Country Music Awards for "Hillbilly Bone." The year 2010 marked Blake finally being recognized for his work. This was his first big award. He had been nominated for the CMA Horizon Award back in 2003, but there had been a long stretch where even nominations were not happening. I couldn't understand it the same way I couldn't understand why it took girls so long to figure out that he was good-looking.

At the May #1 party for "Hillbilly Bone," the Country Music Association donated $10,000 worth of dog bones to the Nashville Humane Society in honor of the success of the song. Just as "Austin" had kickstarted his career, "Hillbilly Bone" did the same for his increased popularity, with a string of #1 hits and numerous awards.

On May 1, rain started falling in Nashville and within thirty-six hours, the city was flooded with almost fourteen inches of water. The Grand Ole Opry stage was underwater by May 3 and eleven souls were lost in the Nashville area alone.

We weren't sure we would be able to have the party that year, as the Wildhorse was also flooded. When we got there on June 10 for the party, they showed us the flood water line in the basement. We were very lucky that they were able to clean it up and be ready in less than six weeks.

At the 2010 Blake Shelton Fan Club Party, Blake took some time out to take requests. The fan club had presented him with his birthday gift, a $30,609 check to LLS, and he decided to grow that amount a little more by allowing those in attendance to make their requests. If he knew the song, he would sing it. If he didn't, he would donate $20. He got some pretty crazy requests and some guests were quite generous, so he was able to add an additional $510 for the Leukemia and Lymphoma Society. Special guests for the evening included Erin Andrews, Dierks Bentley, Laura Bell Bundy, and Frankie Ballard. For some reason I especially remember Erin Andrews backstage. She was the only person sitting on a sofa across the room from me, and she wore cute Greek sandals laced up her legs with either shorts or a short skirt. I had no idea who she was, but I spoke to her. She didn't have much to say, but there were people hovering around her as she proclaimed, "Mama needs some chicken." Someone quickly ran out and got Mama some chicken. It made me smile.

Right after the party, Blake had to get back to touring. He played eighty-four shows in 2010 and seventeen were in July; he was on the road a lot that year. *All About Tonight*'s second release, "Who Are You When I'm Not Looking" (Earl Bud Lee and John Wiggins) was in September with the Trey Fanjoy video premiering in October on GAC. It went on to become the GAC #1 video of the year for 2010. It also marked Blake's third consecutive #1 hit.

On September 28, the Grand Ole Opry reopened four months after the devastating flood with a Country Comes Home concert featuring Brad Paisley, Little Jimmy Dickens, and many others. Blake came out toward the end of the evening to sing "She Wouldn't Be Gone." Then he welcomed Trace Adkins to join him for "Hillbilly Bone." After the song, his good friend Trace put his arm around Blake and started teasing him about "being famous for the Twitter thing" and added, "the Grand Ole Opry sent you a tweet . . . here, look." He handed Blake his cell phone which showed a tweet that was also blown up on the big screen behind them so the crowd could see, "*@blakeshelton, you're invited to join the Grand Ole Opry. See you on 10/23/2010!*" Blake, seldom but now nearly speechless, finally said, "Man, that takes a long time. I know a lot of guys that want this as bad as I have wanted it—forget them for now—I don't know what I ever did in the last year or so to finally turn Nashville's head a little bit, but whatever I did, man, I'm loving this. This moment right here is hands down the highlight of my career. Thank y'all so much. Thank you Grand Ole Opry!"

Between the invite and the induction, Larry and his cousin Farrell Large went on a short run with Blake to shows in Texas and Louisiana. It was the weekend of the Red River Showdown, a football game between longtime rivals, the Oklahoma Sooners and the Texas Longhorns. The guys watched the game on the bus and OU won that year! They tried to meet up annually for a while but it eventually became impossible. Blake isn't on tour constantly anymore, so the timing doesn't usually work.

We remain eternally grateful that Blake asked us to be there for the *big* event of the year, his induction into the Grand Ole Opry. Blake sent a bus to pick up his family and us in Ada's Walmart parking lot. We were all so happy for him that we didn't even think about a nap on the way to Nashville.

There was a party of some of his closest friends and colleagues before the induction. Everyone we expected to see was there, and I can't even begin to name them all. Grand Ole Opry members dropped by to congratulate Blake and welcome him to the family. Little Jimmy Dickens was there wearing a light blue suit with lots of rhinestones and joked, "Blake is so tall that if he fell, he'd be halfway home." Blake felt that Little Jimmy embodied the history of the Grand Ole Opry. Speaking to that close-knit group, Blake related, "Tonight for me is the Nashville dream. Tonight is the pinnacle—the reason that you move to Nashville. If you're me, this is what I wanted from the beginning." Trace said that Blake was his favorite country artist to sing or just hang out with. Blake was so excited to be there and kept asking us if we'd seen this or that. I didn't take any pictures at all, just wanting to soak up the moment. In fact, I was really in a bit of a fog—like it was a dream. There was no question that it was a highlight of his life! As usual, Larry milled around and socialized more than I did. Looking back, I do wish I'd taken at least a few pictures but I was genuinely engrossed in the moment. After the pre-party, we were all ushered into the audience, where they had reserved seats for us. I found myself front and center right between Larry and John Esposito. I sat mesmerized through the entire performance. Priceless!

John Esposito has been the head of Warner Music Nashville (WMN) since 2009, and he appreciates that Blake is a team player, that he wants to see all the artists on the label succeed, and has taken many of them out on tour with him as his opening act. Since first meeting Esposito, I have run into him at several of Blake's shows. It is not uncommon to see him dancing to Blake's music. He is involved—no wonder he has been successful!

On that night, October 23, 2010, Trace Adkins was the one who made the induction, telling Blake, "This is a special night and I'm proud to be a part of it." He then introduced vice president and general manager Pete Fisher, who presented Blake with a fourteen-inch bronze replica of the Grand Ole Opry microphone, mounted on an oak base of wood taken from the Ryman Auditorium when it was remodeled. As he handed him the microphone, Fisher told Blake, "Opry membership is unlike anything else you will ever have. We applaud all you have accomplished and recognize all you have done." Trace concluded with, "Blake Shelton, you are the newest member of the Grand Ole Opry."

Blake spoke to the sold-out Opry audience with heartfelt words, "I was asked what it meant for me to be an Opry member. I didn't have a good answer for that until I walked into this circle tonight and then I knew. It's the same feeling I get when I meet one of my heroes; I'm in awe. To me, the Grand Ole Opry is an artist, and I'm proud to be one of its songs." He added, "I put a lot of thought into what song I would perform as the first one after being made an official member of the Opry. I believe that this song represents how I feel standing on this stage tonight." And then he sang "Home." I wasn't just shedding a tear; they were streaming down my face.

When Blake was nominated for four CMA awards, Warner Music Nashville sent voting members a giant card listing his accomplishments:

> *Blake Shelton . . . is the only male vocalist with two #1 singles this year . . . has had every single released since 2007 be top 10 or better . . . has one of the top 10 most played singles of 2010:* Hillbilly Bone *. . . is changing the way people consume music by releasing two six pak albums in 2010 . . . has made national television headlines with two appearances on* Good Morning America, *three*

appearances on The Today Show, *two appearances on* The Late
Late Show with Craig Ferguson, *and appeared on* Chelsea Lately
and Jimmy Kimmel Live!

Blake won Male Vocalist of the Year and Musical Event of the
Year with Trace Adkins for "Hillbilly Bone." *Yay 2010! Finally!* He
was also nominated for Single of the Year and Music Video of the
Year ("Hillbilly Bone").

It wasn't all about music that year, though. Blake holding a huge
fish graced the cover of the *Oklahoma Fishing Guide 2010*. But it
was definitely the awards that made me so happy—such a long
time coming. He received two CMAs, one ACM, one CMT, and
two ACAs. It just warmed my heart that his peers were finally recognizing him. Everyone was so proud of his success and this was
all icing on the cake. But what's a cake without icing!

Loaded: The Best of Blake Shelton was released in November
and featured fifteen of his greatest hits. It is an understatement
to say that he was excited to have a full album of songs he had
recorded and were recognized by fans. It was just a whole lot
more fun for him to be able to do a concert with songs he himself had recorded and not depend on cover songs, though he still
included some that he loved. It would later be certified platinum by the Recording Industry Association of America (RIAA),
meaning it had sold a million copies.

Blake appeared twice on *The Late Late Show with Craig Fer-
guson* in 2010 promoting "All About Tonight" and "Who Are You
When I'm Not Looking." He also made two appearances on *Jimmy
Kimmel Live,* singing "Kiss My Country Ass" and "Hillbilly Bone."

Because 2010 marked so many of Blake's successes, it had been
a memorable year. He was getting some well-deserved recognition
and had become the newest member of the Grand Ole Opry. He
was enjoying a run of #1 hits and his life seemed to be on the right
track. His All About Tonight tour, which began in 2010, was so
successful that he carried it into 2011.

Reba McEntire had been hosting for several years when she asked Blake to join her as cohost for the Academy of Country Music Awards in 2011; they would share that honor for two years before she walked away after fourteen years as host. Blake chose his friend Luke Bryan to share the duties with him for a couple of years before he called an end to it for himself, leaving Luke to continue forward.

Being a host didn't guarantee any nominations, though, and he didn't get even one from the ACMs in 2011. Good grief! However, he did get the opportunity to sing his newest single release, "Honey Bee" (Rhett Akins and Ben Hayslip), on the award show the day before it was released to radio. As was becoming the norm, it was followed by a video. Trey Fanjoy directed both music videos from the album *Red River Blue,* which was released in July by Warner Bros. Nashville, debuting as the #1 album on the *Billboard* 200 chart. "Honey Bee" went #1 as did "God Gave Me You" (Dave Barnes), which became his fifth consecutive #1 and tenth overall.

Blake won the CMT Male Video of the Year: "Who Are You When I'm Not Looking" and the American Music Award for Favorite Country Male Artist and was nominated for Male Country Artist and Country Single: "Honey Bee" at the Teen Choice Awards. This was good because he was beginning to reach younger audiences in addition to his fan base of older fans. "Hillbilly Bone" received a Grammy nomination for Best Country Collaboration with Vocals.

But that wasn't the biggest thing to happen to Blake that year. *The Voice* premiered April 26 on NBC. A reality television singing competition based on the original show from Holland, its goal in the beginning was to find talent over the age of seventeen not currently signed with a label (now lowered to thirteen).

Contestants are chosen through open auditions across the country and then sing in blind rounds to the four judges who are facing away from them. If a judge likes what they hear, they hit a button and their big red chair turns around. If a contestant gets more than a one chair turn, they get to select their own judge.

At least one chair must turn to move forward. They go through a series of rounds until it is finally narrowed to a winner through audience voting. Through this journey, they are mentored by their judge and another talent brought in by their judge.

Blake and Adam Levine were judges since the inception of the show in 2011 until Adam called it quits in 2019; viewers loved the antics from the two as well as their bromance on the show. The first season, they were joined by CeeLo (Gnarls Barkley) and Christina Aguilera. Other coaches who have filled CeeLo's or Christina's chairs through the seasons include Shakira, Usher, Pharrell Williams, Gwen Stefani (No Doubt), Miley Cyrus, Alicia Keys, Jennifer Hudson, and Kelly Clarkson. Carson Daly has hosted the series from the beginning. To date, Blake, who is the only original judge remaining, has had the most wins and the show remains a favorite on NBC.

Rolling Stone reported June 9, 2011, on how *The Voice* got its start. Mark Burnett, the show's producer, gave Christina, Cee Lo, Adam, and Blake his credit card and sent them to Los Angeles's Soho House for dinner. The next day, Levine called Burnett: "Big mistake. I can't wait for you to see this bill. We just killed your fucking credit card." "But you know what?" Burnett told *Rolling Stone*, "It was worth it." In its debut, *The Voice* blasted to #1 with 11.8 million viewers, a certified smash. Adam Levine said, "Ninety-seven percent of the time I probably would never have considered anything like this, but just because it was such a weird, cool idea, I was really interested right off the bat."

Blake felt much the same way. When they had their first meeting about the show, he was the first one there, then CeeLo, Adam, and finally Christina. Having Christina on board was a big incentive to Blake because she was such a huge star, and if she was interested, wouldn't he be crazy not to be involved too? I think he has enjoyed the show more than he ever thought he would. It must be fulfilling to be able to mentor these great singers and he has helped more than a few with their careers. It is also refreshing that all of the singers presented are good, so judges are able to always be encouraging. The laughs come at the expense of each other, not at the contestants—at least not until they know them better.

Blake and Miranda Lambert were married on May 14, 2011, at the Don Strange Ranch in Boerne, Texas, near San Antonio. The ceremony was held in a barn decorated with lots of sparkly lights and sunshine creeping through the cracks in the building.

Following the ceremony, we all moved to a larger area of the ranch with tables and chairs. Chandeliers hung from trees and little wagons with a variety of food choices dotting the exterior. It was covered by *People* magazine. Guests did not take phones or cameras to the event, and had been kept in the dark about the location by being picked up at several motels by buses and taken there.

We met the Bellamy Brothers on our bus and they were extremely open and interesting. Loved them. At the event, we chose a spot that overlooked everything. Katherine Heigl must have had the same idea we did, as she was in our area. She was wearing a pretty blue summer dress. And we saw Joe Nichols leaning up against a fence behind us, taking in the scenery. It was the first time we had seen him since the party years earlier, so of course we spoke to him.

I missed Debi at one point and asked Patti where she had gone. Patti pointed to the hub of the activity and there was Debi having a little chat with Reba and Kelly Clarkson. It was a big night. Many of Blake's family also sing, and they did that night, as did some of the professionals in attendance, namely Martina McBride and Reba, but the main performer for the evening was the talented Neal McCoy.

Despite all the organization and planning, Patti's evening bag was stolen by a busboy. We had been standing to watch Neal perform and it was taken while our backs were turned. I think he set a tray on top of it, collected empty glasses, and picked it up as he left, hiding it under the tray. The Texas Rangers were on the job and got their man though, and it was recovered along with four others.

The next month at the fan club party, Blake again brought the entire band, opening with "All About Tonight." His featured guests for the evening included Laura Bell Bundy, Nan Kelley, Mel Tillis, and Frankie Ballard, all of whom performed. Fan club member Betty Owens had been the top earner for the LLS donations that year and she presented Blake with a check for almost $18,000 made out to his favorite charity. Nan Kelley was at his side during the presentation.

Mel didn't really plan to perform, but when Blake called him out to meet his fans, he asked for Blake's guitar and sang one of his biggest hits, "I Ain't Never" (Mel Tillis and Web Pierce). Then he commented on Blake, "He's sure a good man, I'll tell you that for sure. I've been in the business here for 56 years. This is a country man right here."

Blake had been on some kind of fishing trip with Mel and some of the other Opry members and he told me that Mel could tell some pretty salty stories. I can only imagine the fun Blake had listening to all their stories. He is a great listener! But he's not the only one with a Mel Tillis story.

After the show, we snaked through the back halls of the Wildhorse until we got to the green room. After a quick chat with Blake, Patti noticed Mel sitting on a couch all alone and felt that she should go say hi. As she approached, Mel stood up to greet her and shake her hand. That's when she saw her sister Debi beelining over to them. Debi is a fairly quiet and reserved person. She doesn't like to make a scene or get into a confrontation of any sort. She is easily embarrassed and doesn't enjoy being the center of attention, the antithesis of Patti. Mel and Patti were on one side of a coffee table and Debi was on the other. She reached across the table to shake his hand as Patti introduced her sister to Mel. That was the moment Patti recalls as a Sam Peckinpah minute. Slowly, Mel started to lean over the coffee table. Debi was smiling as she started to say something. It was then that Mel reached toward her and put a hand on each side of her face. Debi's smile changed to confusion as their faces kept getting closer. Mel was going in for a kiss! Patti enjoyed the whole thing so much that she called it magical, and said she could hear harps playing and birds chirping. It was hilarious. She said she had never in her life seen a tighter lipped kiss. To this day, you can just say "Mel" to Patti and she will start laughing.

The next week after the party, Blake joined Brad Paisley's H2O II: Wetter and Wilder tour. We flew to Nashville on October 6 to meet Blake's bus and go on a run with him to Alabama and Georgia. These mini-trips are always fun for us because there is time to actually visit with him and we always love hearing what is going on in his life.

About that same time, Paramount released a remake of the 1984 classic movie *Footloose*, starring Julianne Hough. Blake had been approached to sing the title song in the new version, a song made famous almost thirty years earlier by Kenny Loggins, who had taken "Footloose" (Kenny Loggins and Dean Pitchford) to #1 for three weeks in 1984. Blake said that he was excited to do the song and chose not to stray far from the original version, adding that it would become a country song automatically, simply by having him sing it. He kept his version in the fun vibe of Loggins's original. The soundtrack included other country artists Whitney Duncan, Hunter Hayes, Big & Rich, Zac Brown, Jana Kramer, and Gretchen Wilson. Ironically, the original movie idea was spawned by an event that happened in Elmore City, Oklahoma, in 1980, which happened to be the school where Larry had taught/coached his first two years in 1967–1969. We went to the movie as soon as we could—wouldn't have missed it for anything.

Excited about Blake winning awards last year, and being nominated for even more this year, Warner Bros. sent out a fold-out of quotes about Blake beginning with "the most important and visible ambassador from Nashville to the American Mainstream." —*The New York Times*; "Blake Shelton, the hottest man in country music right now." —Regis Philbin, *LIVE! With Regis and Kelly*; "Blake

Shelton has been one of country music's biggest stars over the past decade." —*Rolling Stone*; "Shelton's so charming, he could sing his way down a to-do list." —*Entertainment Weekly*; "We now know officially . . . the most interesting man is Blake Shelton." —Music Row.com; and more. The hot song was "Honey Bee," which was his ninth #1 single. The album *Red River Blue* prompted the Associated Press to say, "Shelton adds fuel to the upward trajectory with the best album of his career." Things were looking good.

We flew back to Nashville for the 2011 CMAs. Blake was nominated in five categories: Male Vocalist, Album, Video, Single, and Entertainer. He won Male Vocalist of the Year for the second year in a row! I was texting with his dad who was watching from Ada. Dick loved to text; he probably figured out as I did that it was much easier to get a response from his son through a text as opposed to an actual phone call. I think we all were finding it difficult to truly understand how busy Blake's life was becoming and it would become even busier.

Blake spent that Christmas Eve with his dad in his St. Anthony Hospital room in Shawnee, Oklahoma. The rest of the family carried on with traditions of the past, not realizing how bad Dick would get very soon. In fact, Blake was helping Terrie get his home readied for a homecoming. I think it was fate that father and son spent that time together. It was the pinnacle of quality time.

Blake told *Country Weekly*, "It ended up being dad and I on Christmas Eve, sitting in his hospital room watching *Dumbest Stuff on Wheels* for about four hours on his little TV there in the room. I wouldn't trade that night for anything."

CHAPTER EIGHT

I'LL JUST HOLD ON

December 30, 2011, we went to Winstar Casino in Thackerville, Oklahoma, to catch Blake's last show before beginning the new tour on January 12. The next night, Blake was featured on *NBC's New Year's Eve with Carson Daly*. Add *The Voice* to his almost thirty concerts coming up early the next year to clearly see that he was burning the candle at both ends.

Dick Shelton had been struggling with his health for a few years but it had become much worse. He was spending a lot of time in the hospital in nearby Shawnee, Oklahoma. Having been a smoker for years, he was having more and more difficulty breathing. At one point, he had a sit down with his doctor and told him that if it ever got to the point where he was being kept alive solely by a machine, to pull the plug. He had the same talk with his immediate family. Toward the end of his life, it was becoming more and more obvious that he was not going to be able to survive the problems he was facing.

Blake was in the midst of the tour and had started flying back to Shawnee after every show and flying to the next show the following day. After nearly a week of that, it was beginning to take its toll. We met him coming out of the elevator one day and he looked near exhaustion, not even raising his face to look at anyone until Larry called his name. The time came that the doctor told Dick that the machine was doing all the work and Dick made the decision to end it. He waited until he was able to visit with his family and then asked the doctor to disconnect the life support system. I thought it was the bravest thing I had ever heard. Blake texted me that they had done it and the doctor said it could be a few days. A few hours later he texted me the saddest words he has ever written: "he's gone." January 17, 2012.

The family chose, or maybe Dick had chosen, to have him cremated. They got together one day and spread his ashes at places he held dear: his backyard in Ada, his childhood stomping grounds in Lawton, Oklahoma, and atop a hill on Blake's property in Tishomingo—ashes to ashes. Wife Terrie fashioned a little sanctuary at their home and Blake had a cross placed on a hill at his place in memory of Dick. A wonderful memorial was held in Ada, which featured his favorite songs and pictures of his full life. Many of Blake's Nashville friends, including Reba and Trace, attended to say goodbye to one of the bravest men I've ever known. Rarely a day passes that Larry doesn't mention Dick; he misses their daily talks so much.

Blake's newest party song, "Drink On It" (Jessi Alexander, Rodney Clawson, Jon Randall) was released in January as the third single from *Red River Blue*. It became Blake's sixth consecutive #1 on April 28, exactly eleven years to the day from his first appearance on the chart with "Austin." The next single would be the fourth and final one from this album. "Over" (Paul Jenkins and David Elliot Johnson) was released in May and it was destined to go #1 by September.

Blake had begun his Well Lit and Amplified tour in January and it ran through mid-March, with a total of twenty-seven dates, and then a couple more in April. Dia Frampton, runner up from season 1 of *The Voice*, would be joining Blake on the tour, and season 2 would premiere February 5, right after the Super Bowl. Blake was honored to be asked to sing "America the Beautiful" (Samuel A. Ward: music, 1883; and Katharine Lee Bates: lyrics, 1895) live during the opening of Super Bowl XLVI.

The four original judges from *The Voice* were featured on the cover of *Rolling Stone* magazine on February 16, 2012. Enjoying good rapport from the beginning, Blake truly liked all of the judges.

He told me CeeLo is a genius, Christina takes too much flack for being a diva because she is a woman, and Adam is a jokester.

Blake was recognized with a couple of Grammy nominations in 2012—Best Country Solo Performance: "Honey Bee"; and Best Country Album: *Red River Blue*. He hosted the 47th Annual Academy of Country Music Awards with Reba in April. He was nominated for Entertainer of the Year and Male Vocalist of the Year, and won the award for Male Vocalist. Right after he didn't win the entertainer award, he brought out Lionel Richie to sing "You Are" (Lionel Richie, Brenda Harvey Richie), a duet the two recorded for Richie's *Tuskegee* album that had just been released. Also, the performance served as a reminder to fans that *Lionel Richie and Friends—In Concert* would be airing on CBS April 13.

He won the CMT Teddy Award for the Best Flirting Video: "Honey Bee." The People's Choice Awards nominated him for Favorite Male Artist and Favorite Country Artist, CMT Music Awards for Video of the Year: "God Gave Me You," Male Video of the Year: "God Gave Me You," and CMT Performance of the Year: "Footloose." The Teen Choice Awards nominated him in three categories—Male Country Artist; Country Song: "God Gave Me You"; and Male Artist.

In August, Blake invited us to fly with him to a show in St. Paul, Minnesota, the home of Blake's #1 fan Connie Schultz. I had never flown on a private jet before and was excited to join him on that rather long flight. We picked him up in Tishomingo and drove to the airport in Durant, Oklahoma. As we were walking toward the plane, Blake noticed a wire that tethered the plane and said to the pilot, "I told you to get that fixed. It will make her (pointing at me) nervous to have the wing wired up like that." He never misses an opportunity to try to worry me about something stupid and has learned I often fall for it—but not that time. I was excited about the trip because it gave us plenty of time to visit, especially on the way there when everyone was wide awake. There were tacos available on the plane, but Larry had stopped at a fast food place and got fried chicken for Blake. I enjoyed the tacos and the company.

In September we were able to see another Blake show in Oklahoma at Winstar Casino, part of Blake's Well Lit and Amplified tour. I picked up one of the huge programs with lots of pictures to commemorate that tour.

When we attended the CMAs in 2012, it was with a heavy heart. I wouldn't be able to text Dick that year and see him get so excited over his son's wins. And Dorothy and Dick's boy won big that year! Blake won Entertainer of the Year, Male Vocalist of the Year, and Song of the Year for "Over You," an award that goes to songwriters, for the song that his dad had encouraged him to write several years before. It felt like Dick was there and Blake commented about him in his acceptance speech. The only nomination he didn't win was Single of the Year for "God Gave Me You." Larry and I decided that those wins could never be topped and that going forward we would stop going to the actual shows and watch them from our recliners back in Ada. But what a year! Bittersweet and wonderful!

Hendricks and Rowan teamed up to coproduce Blake's first Christmas album, *Cheers, It's Christmas*, which was released in early October. It included "Time for Me to Come Home," which Blake cowrote with his mother, Dorothy Shackleford, who also was a featured vocalist on the song. Another special song was "The Very Best Time of the Year," cowritten by Blake and Trypta-Phunk (band members Rob Byus, Tracy Broussard, and Beau Tackett), who were featured voices as well. Having always loved Christmas songs, an album was something he always wanted to do. The television special was a plus.

Music from the album was highlighted on *Blake Shelton's Not So Family Christmas*, an NBC hour-long special on December 3. The show also featured Kelly Clarkson, Dorothy Shackleford, Miranda Lambert, and Reba McEntire. It was full of the Christmas music Blake loves and the hilarious sketches that he enjoys. The year ended better than it began.

GACs *Backstory* from 2009 was updated and broadcast as episode 3, season 3, in December 2012. Blake was interviewed and made the statement, "If I am Male Vocalist of the Year, that must mean that I'm one of those people now that gets to decide if it moves forward and if it moves on. Country music has to evolve in order to survive. Nobody wants to listen to their grandpa's music." Blake clearly understood that each generation wants music to call their own and that the young kids were buying music now and not the last generation, who he lovingly referred to as old farts, and that it didn't matter that a few jackasses were complaining that it wasn't country. Of course, it sounded much worse quoted out of context. A couple of older artists had fun with that idea. Willie Nelson took advantage of maybe not having evolved by renaming his tour the Old Farts and Jackass tour. Ray Stevens said, "All I want to know is how he found out the title to my next single because it's been a closely guarded secret . . . it will be available on vinyl or 8-track." I love their sense of humor! But some of the Opry members were truly offended and finally, when Ray Price voiced a negative opinion on the subject, Blake posted a series of tweets that read in their entirety, "Whoa! I heard I offended one of my all-time favorite artists Ray Price. The truth about my statement was and still is how we as the new generation of country artists have to keep reinventing country music to keep it popular just exactly the way Mr. Price did by pushing the boundaries with his records. 'For the Good Times' [Kris Kristofferson], perfect example with the introduction of a bigger orchestrated sound in country music. It was new and awesome! I absolutely have no doubt I could have worded it better as always and I apologize to Mr. Price and any other heroes of mine that it may have offended. Country music is my life and its future and past is important to me. I'll put my love and respect and knowledge about it up against anybody out there—anybody!"

Two days later, Ray Price accepted Blake's apology personally and a week later, Blake met with him prior to Price's performance in Durant, Oklahoma. Ray invited Blake onto his bus for a visit and the battle was over.

January saw the release of "Sure Be Cool if You Did" (Rodney Clawson, Jimmy Robbins, Chris Tompkins) from the new album *Based on a True Story*, which would be out by the end of March, right after that first single went #1. On the same day the album was released, so was "Boys 'Round Here" (Rhett Akins, Dallas Davidson, Craig Wiseman) which would go #1 by the end of June. Then in July fans welcomed "Mine Would Be You" (Jessi Alexander, Connie Harrington, Deric Ruttan), which became the next #1 in November, sending all three singles released in 2013 to the top of the *Billboard* chart. Blake was truly on a roll that was not going to end anytime soon. *Based on a True Story* became the ninth best-selling album in the United States in 2013.

For a while, Hoda Kotb had gushed over a celebrity crush with Blake on her morning show. Coincidentally, she had just got a new puppy and was debating naming it Blake when he called into the show on March 28. That cinched it and Blake became a part of her family. Later that evening, Blake Shelton, Jimmy Fallon, Nick Offerman, and Chris Tartaro appeared on *Late Night with Jimmy Fallon* performing as the Chickaneers with an all-clucking version of "Ho Hey" (Wesley Schultz, Jeremy Fraites), a song by the Lumineers. The reviews were great and everyone loved their performance. It was becoming clear to everyone what we had known all along: there are many layers to Blake Shelton.

Blake was so hot that at some point, he accidentally set some of his land on fire and had to call out the Johnston County, Oklahoma, local volunteer fire departments. It made him realize that they needed help themselves, so he scheduled a benefit performance at nearby Murray State College in March. The event sold out quickly. It was done old school by calling in or showing up to buy a ticket so I started calling. I told Blake I hit redial so many times that I fell asleep three times during the two or three hours when I tried to get my tickets. I still couldn't buy tickets. We often

Blake in front of famed Douglas Corner Café, where we held early fan club parties.

Blake's first performance at the Grand Ole Opry. PHOTO BY DEBORAH LARGE

Blake and I celebrating at a summer concert on Nashville's Broadway.

Look at that smile!
PHOTO BY PATRICIA JOHNSON

He thinks he can get another sticker for his guitar case right there.

Admiration for Earl Thomas Conley is clearly written on Blake's face.

Blake and Larry returning from a trip to Tunica, Mississippi.

Finally cutting off that Sasquatch hair because it was too dang hot!

Blake trying to operate the exercise chair while he talks to his mother on the phone live at a fan club party. PHOTO BY ANNA MOSER ORF

Posing for a picture with Patti backstage at a concert.

Larry, Blake, and I at the Country Music Hall of Fame celebrating the Blake Shelton Exhibit.

Accepting membership into the Grand Ole Opry.
PHOTO BY ANNA MOSER ORF

A celebratory hug at the after party when Blake did his first full-fledged concert at the Ryman Auditorium.

Larry was honored to make the introductory speech when Blake was inducted into the Oklahoma Hall of Fame. PHOTO BY JOE OWNBEY / OWNBEYPHOTOGRAPHY.COM

Blake surprised me with a visit when I was in the hospital for tests.

Debi, Patti, me, and Blake grabbing a selfie at Madison Square Garden during rehearsal for his concert.

Blake with me and Larry at The Voice.

Gwen and Blake backstage at one of the California concerts when we went out on the road with him just a couple of weeks before COVID-19 shut everything down.

Behind scenes at filming of The Voice *live from Tishomingo, Oklahoma, during pandemic.*

accepted complimentary concert tickets, but always paid at charity events. We went over to see him before the concert and he brought his pet kangaroo. I got to feed it, so cute! Then he insisted we go backstage to watch the show. I felt so guilty that we hadn't paid that I sent one of the fire departments a check the next day. Proceeds for the show went to a scholarship fund at Murray and volunteer fire departments at Ravia, Milburn, and Tishomingo.

The Academy of Country Music presented Blake with the Gene Weed Special Achievement Award, which acknowledges unprecedented, unique, and outstanding achievement by a country music performer. His friend Steve Wariner made the presentation. There were many reasons he deserved the award, including the fact that Blake had brought country music to prime time television through his influence on the hit reality talent show *The Voice*.

The Academy of Country Music nominated Blake Shelton for Entertainer of the Year and he won for Song of the Year: "Over You." Blake continued to host the ACMs and invited Luke Bryan to join him since Reba had decided to retire from her hosting duties. He received several nominations: People's Choice Awards for Favorite Male Artist and Favorite Country Artist, Kids' Choice Awards for Favorite Male Singer, and American Music Awards for Favorite Country Male Artist. The American Country Awards nominated him for Artist of the Year and Male Artist of the Year and he won their Album of the Year: *Based on a True Story*; Single by a Male Artist: "Sure Be Cool if You Did"; and the Great American Country Music Video of the Year for "Sure Be Cool if You Did." He also won the CMT Music Awards Male Video of the Year for "Sure Be Cool if You Did." And he received another Grammy Award nomination for "Over."

But then tragedy struck again when, on the afternoon of May 20, an EF5 tornado struck Moore, Oklahoma, killing twenty-four people and injuring 377 others. The devastation was tremendous. Ten of those killed were children, including seven who were at school. Blake's sister Endy had lived in Moore but had moved before the storm. My nephew, Barry Cash, and his family were very close but had a cellar that was overcrowded with everyone they could squeeze inside. They were on the edge of the storm and had minimal damage. Lucky! Blake was heartbroken over the events of that horrid day and he reacted immediately. He felt he could and should do something to help. In just over a week, he put together an event to again help his home state, which had more than its fair share of disasters in recent years.

On May 29, 2013, Blake hosted a relief benefit concert, *Healing in the Heartland,* which was televised on NBC. More than $6 million in ticket sales and pledges for the one-hour event was raised to benefit victims of the tornado. Blake featured Usher, among others, for the televised portion. Blake pulled off the benefit with enormous success.

I was there when a girl whose mother had been killed in the tornado and who had been given a scholarship to college from proceeds of the benefit came onto the bus, and Blake handed her an extra thousand dollars for spending money at college. He does little things like that all the time that are not publicized.

Blake loved owning land more than anything because according to him, "They aren't making it anymore," and he had bought another property in the Tishomingo area, but not near his farm. We had been down before and Blake had taken us out on the rough dirt road in his pickup as we laughed at him for flipping off a particularly mean emu. Since then he had built a lodge on the property, complete with a big lake, several cabins, an outdoor cooking area, mini-saloon, and so forth, but we hadn't seen it. We drove there in June. His family was all there too and they were cooking macaroni and cheese along with some other things. Anyway, we all sat around and ate and visited.

Blake had a chair he had bought after seeing one in the green room at the *Chelsea Handler* show. It wrapped around both arms and legs and massaged every inch of your body. I could have stayed there for hours. Blake said he had some guys down for a hunting trip and one of them never went hunting, just chose to stay in that chair. He also laughed about Adam Levine's visit. He said Adam didn't like much about the country, especially the grasshoppers.

Finally, Blake said it was getting dark and for us to hurry, that he had something he wanted us to see. We went outside and there was a bus convertible of sorts painted with zebra stripes. There were comfortable chairs inside and we all climbed aboard; Larry and I got at the very back facing the front. Blake was driving and entertaining. Endy and her kids and Dorothy and Mike were loaded in on the sides, all laughing. There was a picture of Blake (from the Jimmy Fallon show when they did the parody of "Ho Hey") wearing a chicken suit painted on the window of the passenger side up front. There were no windows in the rest of the bus since the entire top had been cut off to the bottom of the windows. As we took off, Blake picked up a microphone and started giving us an over-exaggerated history of the lodge and telling us about his animals in the funny way only he can do. It was like having a tour guide through a wild life ride at Disneyland or something, plain fun. I hope Blake Shelton never grows up!

Blake kicked off his Ten Times Crazier tour in July 2013, promoting *Based on a True Story*. Working around his busy schedule, he performed at sixty-two shows in two legs of the tour, between then and the end of June 2015.

Blake's entourage raked in a good number of awards in 2013. Winners of CMA's Standing Room Only (SRO) awards for outstanding professional achievement within the touring industry that year included: manager Narvel Blackstock, tour manager Kevin Canady, front of house (FOH) engineer Jeff "Pig" Parsons, monitor engineer Brad Baisley, production manager Art Rich, and coach/truck driver Kelly Beck.

The year continued to bring Blake more awards, too. At the CMAs, he was nominated in five categories including Entertainer of the Year; Musical Event of the Year: "Boys 'Round Here"; and Music Video of the Year: "Boys 'Round Here"; and he took home

Album of the Year: *Based on a True Story*; as well as a fourth consecutive win for Male Vocalist of the Year. Larry and I were watching the show that year from our easy chairs in front of the television, both kicked back enjoying it more up-close than ever. It was the first year in many that we hadn't attended the live performance. After the landslide of wins Blake took home in 2012, we had decided to stay home. Toward the end of one of his acceptance speeches, Blake said, "and I don't think I've ever thanked Larry and Carol Large." Well, we were shocked for a couple of seconds, then stared at each other—what did he just say? And then our phone started ringing off the hook. We just weren't expecting it. Blake has thanked us in liner notes on every studio album he has done, so we knew he appreciated us, but it caught us off guard to hear him say it in front of millions on live television. We love Blake unconditionally and he knows that. Yes, we have tried to be supportive of his career since he was a teenager, moved him to Nashville in 1994 and moved ourselves in 1996, did our best to keep him motivated, and all that. But here is the bottom line: we are retired now and Blake continues to keep our lives exciting. He takes us with him on the road at least one weekend of every tour, invites us to special events, and texts me regularly about what he is doing. He even offers the use of his home for vacations from time to time. We have been so many places and done so many things that would not have been possible for retired educators without him. We thank him!

Following a concert in Tulsa, Blake donated $20,000 to the Oklahoma Department of Wildlife Conservation to support their outdoor education programs. He felt their efforts were an important way to get kids back outdoors.

At Christmas, he surprised us with two platinum albums: *Red River Blue* and *Based on a True Story*. While most Blake-related things can be found in my home office, those two albums proudly hang in our living room.

"Doin' What She Likes" (Wade Kirby, Phil O'Donnell) was the next single, debuting on January 6, 2014, and going on to become Blake's next #1, breaking Brad Paisley's record of consecutive #1s. Nielsen Broadcast Data Systems has tracked #1 singles on country charts since January 1990, and Paisley had a string of ten consecutive top charting songs from 2005–2009.

Blake went on to have his fifth #1 from the same album with "My Eyes" (Andrew Dorff, Tommy Lee James, Josh Osborne), the song featuring Gwen Sebastian, a season 2 *The Voice* contestant who had been eliminated before the live shows and that he had hired as a backup singer.

In late February, Blake announced the upcoming dates for the 2014 Ten Times Crazier tour and I decided to surprise Larry by flying him to the Chicago show at Wrigley Field in July. It was supposed to be a birthday gift, but it bothered him that I wasn't going, so I told him I'd rather go to the one at Madison Square Garden with Debi and Patti the following month. He was good to go. He flew out there and enjoyed the show which was filled to capacity with over forty thousand fans. It was on that trip that Blake told Larry he had been selected to be inducted into the Oklahoma Hall of Fame and that he wanted Larry to make the induction. Needless to say, Larry was overwhelmed, delighted, and honored. He flew back with Blake, and Debi and I picked him up about three o'clock in the morning at Ardmore. After the usual round of hugs, Blake got in his old truck that had the back bumper wired up and drove home by himself. I remember thinking how surreal it must be for him to perform in front of that many people and less than six hours later be in an old truck by himself driving down an Oklahoma dirt road. Needless to say, Larry came back with stories to tell!

On March 15, 2014, Blake joined a bevy of stars to wish the Grand Ole Opry House a happy fortieth anniversary. Odd the things you remember, but I had always thought it was so cool that John Anderson, who made "Swingin'" (John Anderson, Lionel

Delmore) famous back in 1983, had worked as a roofer on the GOO house just six years earlier while he was trying to make his mark in country music. Also, President Nixon had impressed the first audience there with his yoyo tricks.

The big show for me that year was Madison Square Garden in August, and I started making plans. It was decided that it would be a girls' trip: me, Debi, and Patti. David and Larry could stay home with the dogs. We booked our flights and a hotel near Times Square. Kevin Canady had sent us access passes and our plan was to see some Broadway shows, shop, and see Blake.

Kevin had also snagged us some tickets to see *Late Night with Jimmy Fallon* on Thursday night so we got to town early for that and it was well worth it. One of the producers from *The Voice* met us with gift bags and ushered us to our seats. I wish I had written down her name because I have forgotten and she went out of her way to make us happy. Fallon's guests that night were Julia Roberts (who was a good sport playing one of his silly games where they got to hit each other in the face with big blow up balls), Andy Cohen, and comedian Ron Funches (who we ran into on the sidewalk outside as we left the show). We told him his routine was hilarious and he thanked us—very friendly guy. We enjoyed watching him on *Undateables* a couple of years later.

But the main reason for the trip was Blake, so we went to the Garden early Friday afternoon, August 1, to catch sound check and had a heck of a time getting past security guards. First they sent us out and around to another entry, but that didn't work because they sent us right back to the front again. We had our all-access passes but they wouldn't work. Finally, totally frustrated I said, "Do I need to call Blake and have him come out here to verify we are OK to go in?" and the guy hesitantly allowed us to go inside. Good thing, because Blake rarely answers his phone.

Sound check was going on and we stopped to talk to a few people we knew and waved at Blake before finding a spot to sit and watch the rehearsal. When they were finished, Blake came out to visit a little bit and hear a history lesson from Debi (who was excited beyond belief) on who all had performed there. She let him know that in her opinion, it was a huge deal to play where Led Zeppelin and Elvis had once played. I decided to get a selfie but am simply not good with a camera, so Blake grabbed it and held his long arm out so he could get us all in the camera's eye. After a few laughs, we left and went shopping, then back to the room to freshen up for the show.

Blake opened the show by shouting, "I'm a country singer. How the hell did I end up playing at Madison Square Garden? I am freaking out!" He had the crowd in the palm of his hand. Afterward we went backstage. Reba and a couple of her friends from Franklin, Tennessee, were back there. I don't take a lot of pictures, preferring to bask in the moment, but had been told to get some pictures this time. I had known Reba a little since she was in high school and asked if I could get a picture with her; of course she obliged. Blake saw us posing and yelled across the small room, "Carol, leave Reba alone!" Debi settled in at a table and talked to Reba almost the entire time and I visited with her friends. We hadn't known them when we lived in Franklin but it was something we had in common and they were very nice. We talked about Broadway shows and what we were going to see. We had decided on *Hedwig and the Angry Inch*, a rock musical starring Neil Patrick Harris, and *A Gentleman's Guide to Love and Murder*, which had just won the Tony Award for Best Musical. We went back through Times Square and checked out all the entertainment going on there, and then headed back to our rooms to settle down and visit a little before going to sleep. (Times Square had the Naked Cowboy, SpongeBob Square Pants, and any other character you could think up selling pictures with them, just a crazy space, like a city version of Venice Beach in California). Imagine our dismay when we realized I hadn't checked my email and missed the invitation to the after party. The girls were a little put out with me. Heck, I thought Reba was the after party.

Blake appeared on *Late Night with Jimmy Fallon* along with *The Voice* judge Gwen Stefani and they did a lip-sync contest. My favorite was Blake's version of Taco's "Puttin' on the Ritz" (Irving Berlin). Blake showed off his personality by carrying a drink that he put aside to do a soft shoe in his boots, and his lips were perfectly synced. His funny facial expressions were those I had become so used to through the years. A year after Adam Levine had topped the list and made the cover of *People's Sexiest Man Alive* issue and sent Blake a house-sized copy of that cover to Oklahoma, Blake also made the list, if not the cover, in 2014.

"Neon Light" (Andrew Dorff, Mark Irwin, Josh Kear), which would continue Blake's #1 streak, was released in August as the first single from the next album. *Bringing Back the Sunshine* could be found online and on shelves by the end of September. The video for "Neon Light" was directed by Cody Kern.

The next month Ada decided to celebrate Blake's new album, *Bringing Back the Sunshine,* which featured the old Ada *witch hat* water tower on the cover, with a release party on East Main between Mississippi and East Central University in the area known as the arts district. There was an official dedication of that part of Main (Mississippi Avenue to ECU) as Blake Shelton Boulevard. An ECU art class had painted a mural on the side of a building at the corner that featured prominent artists from Ada including Mae Axton and Blake Shelton. Sara Jane Johnson, who was heading up the event for the city of Ada, worked very hard to bring the successful event to fruition. They had a huge yellow balloon tunnel, a kid zone where kids could get their faces painted or play in bounce houses, a mechanical bull, food trucks, music, a Blake look-a-like contest that included Dorothy as one of the judges, and a talent show hosted by Blake's good friend Nan Kelley (who had been flown in for the event thanks to the Chickasaw Nation), and the area was packed shoulder to shoulder with people. Everyone was disappointed that Blake wasn't there despite being told in advance that he could not be there . . . they sort of didn't believe that. Sara Jane had come up with a giant blow-up screen and Blake had recorded a video thanking everyone, which was a big hit.

Blake was in the midst of the Ten Times Crazier tour and on the road a lot when he took time to return to Ada for a *60 Minutes* interview with Norah O'Donnell in 2014. He drove her around town and answered all her questions. We met up with them at the McSwain Theatre where he did the sit-down portion of the interview. I enjoyed meeting Norah and it was obvious that she enjoyed meeting Blake. While they were driving around the high school, he ran into Patti and David's niece, Devanee Simmons. Blake said, "Say hi to David for me." Norah got a kick out of the fact that he was still just an Ada guy. He told her that he thought people liked country music at least partially because they identify with the singer. They talked about Blake's songs and that he didn't write most of his hits. He agreed that out of the two or three hundred songs he had written, he was only proud of about fifteen of them. She mentioned that he sang a lot about girls and drinking and he agreed that he did because he liked those things. They talked about the funny songs too, and the dark ones, and that he was on a roll with consecutive #1 hits. Of course he talked about losing his brother Richie and dad Dick. The interview truly gave viewers a look into what it would be like to be Blake Shelton.

The biggest actual surprise of Blake's career, to me at least, was when Barbra Streisand asked him to do a duet, "I'd Want It to Be You" (Steve Dorff, Jay Landers, Bobby Tomberlin), on her album *Partners*. When I visited with Blake about it, I asked him what she was like; I had always been a huge fan of her music and the movie *A Star Is Born* starring her and Kris Kristofferson. In fact, I had often fantasized about Blake doing a fourth remake of that movie cast in the KK role. (Drat you Bradley Cooper.) He said that he still hadn't met her; the song was done in the studio with separate vocals. She had already recorded her part and was in London listening on the phone as he recorded his. When asked by *People* magazine if it was nerve-racking he replied, "Hell yes, it was nerve-wracking! I kept saying 'Thank you, thank you for thinking of me' . . . She was very sweet about it. I'm still speechless." He said he thought she liked it; she sent him a piece of crystal as a thank you gift. The album's debut on the top of the charts made Streisand the first act to achieve number one albums in each of the last six decades. Wow!

At the CMAs in 2014, Blake was nominated for Entertainer of the Year and took home the Male Vocalist of the Year award for a record-tying fifth consecutive win. Another Okie, Vince Gill, had held the record since the early 1990s. Blake had again hosted the ACMs with Luke Bryan in 2014 before he left hosting duties to Luke and Dierks Bentley. He received five nominations (Song: "Mine Would Be You"; Album: *Based on a True Story*; Vocal Event: "Boys 'Round Here"; Entertainer; Male Vocalist) but no wins.

He was also nominated for a Grammy for Best Country Solo Performance: "Mine Would Be You"; and Best Country Album: *Based on a True Story*. At the iHeartRadio Music Awards, two of the five nominations for Country Song of the Year were for Blake: "Boys 'Round Here" and "Mine Would Be You." He won for "Boys 'Round Here." He was again nominated for Favorite Male Singer by the Kids' Choice Awards and the People's Choice Awards nominated him in three categories: Favorite Male Artist, Favorite Country Artist, and Favorite Album: *Based on a True Story*.

Ashley Monroe was featured on the next single, "Lonely Tonight" (Brent Anderson, Ryan Hurd), and it also went to the top of the charts, leaving us all wondering how long this amazing string of hits would persist. Don't get me wrong; we loved it! Blake was breaking records, winning awards, being viewed by millions on television. He was beginning to surpass even my expectations!

The Oklahoma Hall of Fame induction came soon and Larry was happy for Blake and couldn't believe he had asked him to be a part of it—definitely one of the highlights of his life. Larry wore a tie every day as a school administrator and when he retired, he got rid of all his dress clothes, swearing to never wear them again. He became a blue jeans, casual shirt, cap guy! Former students and teachers often don't recognize him. So we headed down to Black's

Mens Wear, where he had bought clothes as a teen and throughout his life, to order a tuxedo. On November 13, 2014, Larry did an outstanding job inducting Blake into this esteemed group of Oklahoma honorees. It was televised and many of his former students and friends saw it. He made his speech about Blake, honoring the guidelines he had been given and refusing the prompter. There is nothing in this world easier for him to talk about than Blake. As he put the ribbon around Blake's neck, Blake had to lean way down and then he gave Larry the best hug I've ever seen. We were seated at a table right up front and I made a couple of new friends that night: Bob Burke, a former inductee who is well known as an attorney/author, and Edna Mae Holden, another attorney whose husband, Harold T. Holden (Western artist), was being inducted that night.

When he gave his acceptance speech, Blake talked about everyone there. He made his mom laugh and the crowd could tell it was his laugh too. He insisted I say the alphabet which I was able to do in two and a half seconds normally (you can pick out a letter and hear it if you listen closely), but that was the last thing I was expecting and I couldn't pull it off. He said, "Well, that sucks." He talked about Larry having so many stories and one that he particularly liked was when he and a friend had stopped at a little roadside bar in eastern Oklahoma to get something and saw an old gun hanging over the bar. They (Larry and Rocky Stone) asked the owner if he would hold it and act like he was chasing them out of the establishment to scare us (me and Margaret Stone). The guy went along with it and successfully scared us, except a trucker passed by about that time and, thinking it was for real, swerved a little off the road. Blake said that he had gone in a ditch and of course the audience caught their breath, making Larry wish he hadn't exaggerated quite so much. After making fun of each and every one of us, Blake also noted that it was the anniversary of his brother's death and he couldn't help thinking that maybe Richie had something to do with the honor. It was a great night and Endy honored us with a photo collage of the evening for Christmas that year to commemorate it.

CHAPTER NINE

BRINGING BACK
THE SUNSHINE

I have been a huge fan of *Saturday Night Live* (*SNL*), the late-night comedy show created by Lorne Michaels, since its inception on NBC, October 11, 1975. I had told Blake for years and years that when he got on that show, I had to be there! So when he told me that he would not only be hosting but would also be the musical guest on January 24, 2015 (my birthday), I was beyond thrilled! *Beyond*! Blake said that he would be very busy and wouldn't have time to spend with us before the show but he would get tickets for all of us: me, Larry, Debi, Patti, and David. We had never all taken a trip together before, but everyone found a place for their dogs for a few days and we booked a flight. We decided to stay away from Times Square that time and opted for a small hotel close to Rockefeller Center. It was across the street from the television studio, so we were able to walk there.

Arriving early as usual, we were given our credentials and soon led to our seats, which were located in front of where the band and Blake would be performing. The *SNL* band and stage was located to our right. I sat there wondering if Blake was nervous because it was such an iconic show and *live*. Knowing he is naturally funny, I had said a little prayer that they utilize that to the benefit of him and the show. As the time drew near, I almost held my breath until I heard the announcer cry *Blake Shelton*! He bounded down those familiar steps, teasing the crowd to think of him as the country Justin Bieber, talking about watching *Hee Haw* as a kid, and progressed into a sketch with the cast members, teaching them about country humor.

He was involved in several sketches: a parody of *The Bachelor* called *Farm Hunk*, a parole hearing for a cannibal, a heckler at a magic show, a member of a country band with cast members Aidy Bryant and Kate McKinnon (who says recording this stupid song was her favorite moment from season 40) in an over-the-top stereotypical music video for "Wishin' Boot" (Chris Kelly, Sarah Schneider), and a few others. In between the acting, Blake and the band performed two songs, "Boys 'Round Here" and "Neon Light." It was fascinating to watch how the show worked behind the scenes. When Blake finished a sketch or song and they went to commercial, someone would come out, grab his hand, and drag him off for a wardrobe change as the stage hands set up for the next sketch. While he was standing to the side of the set below us getting ready for *Farm Hunk*, he turned that blond-wigged head around and searched the audience with his eyes until he spotted us and a small grin passed his face. A time or two, some of the sets were in front of us and we had to watch the monitor to see what the television viewers were seeing. They take advantage of every square inch of space and everyone knew exactly where they were supposed to be. It worked like a well-oiled machine and in the midst of all the organized confusion, producer Lorne Michaels slowly walked around looking over everyone and everything. Very impressive!

After the show, we were invited to an after party several blocks away, so we went back to the hotel and freshened up a little before catching a taxi to that event. Most of Blake's band was in the relatively small hangout so we knew them and Blake's management team and some others. There was a lot of Nashville there that night actually. Mary Ann McCready, Blake's business manager, introduced me to a couple of people and helped make me feel comfortable in a strange place, and Patti thinks she was the one who snapped a picture of me with Kate McKinnon. I was determined to meet Aidy Bryant, Kate McKinnon, and Leslie Jones, and I did. They were all very nice and probably laughed at my Okie accent after I walked away. I wouldn't expect any less. We sat at a table beside Colin Jost and Jay Pharoah, but I never got up my nerve to speak to them. We just nibbled on the snacks and looked around in disbelief that we were actually there.

Lorne Michaels, Blake, and Vanessa Bayer were sitting in a booth against the back wall and I looked up just in time to see Debi joining them. She said Blake introduced her to Michaels by saying, "She has watched the show since the beginning" and she quickly added something like, "I was a baby in my crib." It was the highlight of her evening. Blake's appearance was season 40, episode 12, and it became the second top-rated show of the season, with only the Chris Rock/Prince episode drawing more viewers.

As we were leaving the party, I told Blake that it was my most memorable birthday ever. He said, "It's your birthday? Here!" handing me a bag someone had given him and inside was a jar of moonshine that we knew wasn't going to fly home with us. We don't drink the stuff anyway which is probably why he handed it to me. When we got back to our hotel, we gave it to the desk clerk and he seemed pretty pleased with his new acquisition. It was a very small hotel and we had gotten acquainted with him, told him why we were in town, and he had been helpful with suggestions on where to shop, eat, and that sort of thing. It was a great time!

We left a day before Patti and David and were concerned about their flight out because a major winter storm was moving in on New York City. As it turned out, they made it out on the last flight.

Later I saw Leslie Jones on Andy Cohen's show on Bravo and he asked her who her favorite celebrity had been on *SNL*? She quickly said (and I paraphrase) *hands down, Blake Shelton with all of us*. I was not surprised but I was pleased that they liked Blake as much as I liked them and Blake.

Two short weeks later we headed to Dallas's AT&T Stadium (home of Dallas Cowboys) for the United Way of Metropolitan Dallas 90th Anniversary Celebration concert. We took good friends Barbara and Gil Ragland with us and got there early, which was good as the crowd was huge. *The Voice* coaches, Usher and Blake, were coheadlining the event. Blake came out and did a thirty-minute segment, then Usher, and then they teamed up for a few songs. It was especially fun for the audience when Blake did one of Usher's songs and then Usher did one of his. You could tell the two enjoyed each other and got along well. They repeated that sequence and ended up singing "With a Little Help from My Friends," a song written by John Lennon and Paul McCartney, but made famous by Joe Cocker. They were joined on stage by everyone involved in making the show a success including Usher's dancers and Blake's dancers (the Dallas Cowboys Cheerleaders) and Troy Aikman, among many others.

Shortly thereafter, Blake called and asked if we wanted to come to the ACM Awards, which would be held at the AT&T stadium in April rather than Las Vegas, where they were normally held. We passed, which is something we rarely do. Had we realized it was the fiftieth anniversary of that award show, we probably would have gone. Still, it made us feel good that he thought of us. Blake is loyal to a fault and if nothing else, I hope that comes through in these stories I share with you.

The third single release from *Bringing Back the Sunshine*, "Sangria" (Jess Leary, Anthony Smith), came out in April and the fourth, "Gonna" (Luke Laird, Craig Wiseman), in August. Both went to the top of the charts! I am beginning to realize that Blake is a superstar of a magnitude far beyond my comprehension. When we are visiting with him, he is still the same kid that moved to Nashville, with the same silly annoyances we all, as human beings, have and he still likes to do the same things he has always done, absolutely no difference there.

It is not uncommon to get a text from Blake out of the blue asking a nonsensical question and the two of us bantering back and forth, always leaving me wondering what in the world prompted that. But I love it! And, if you see him with his cell phone on live telecasts of *The Voice*, he is actually texting comments, usually during commercials. On one season, he had a team member who made it pretty far and I wasn't feeling it. After one of his performances, I texted Blake and said, "What in the world is America seeing that I don't get; is it just me?" He immediately quipped, "Yes, it's just you!" Typical Blake.

Things were rolling along as usual the first half of the year—and then, out of the blue, on Saturday, June 13, after a brisk walk around Wintersmith Park in steaming heat, I went home, grabbed a bottle of water and sat down to call my cousin, Janice Smith. Larry had gone to a school class reunion at nearby Fittstown and I was trying to cool off. As I was kicked back in a recliner visiting with Janice, my right leg kept falling off the foot rest. I would put it back and it would happen again. Finally, I reached down to touch my leg and realized it was partially numb, and as I checked my arm and face, they too were numb, just on the right side. I told Janice that I thought I'd call Debi and have her come over and take me to the emergency room.

While I was waiting for her, I went to a mirror and did all the stuff they tell you to do if you think you might be having a stroke. I seemed to be OK other than the numbness and even it wasn't so bad that I couldn't walk. Debi took me to the hospital, which was no longer known as Valley View, having been bought out by Mercy. They did a few tests and decided to admit me. It was the beginning of a weekend and they couldn't do some of the tests they wanted until Monday, so they would just monitor me until then.

The next day, Blake surprised me by strolling into my room. I didn't even know he was in the state, but he had happened to be at his place in Tishomingo when Patti sent him a text letting him know I was in the hospital. He tickled me because he had muddy boots from working in the dirt, something he loves to do. Nurses kept popping in to check on me even more than usual, so Blake finally told them if they would give us some visiting time he would stop and do pictures or whatever they wanted on his way out, which he did. Debi happened to be in the room too, and of course

Larry, so we all had an enjoyable visit for a couple of hours. It was coincidental that Reba's brother, Pake McEntire, was in the same small hospital at the same time, so Larry and Blake stopped by his room for a visit on the way out. Pake had earlier had a serious stroke and was recovering, doing some rehabilitation in Mercy; I'm happy to say he seems to have fully recovered.

I was feeling fine. In fact, once the numbing left, I never had a problem again. I found out that I was in pretty good health as they did every test they could think of during the next couple of days until they released me to go home. It is getting more and more difficult to have one-on-one time with Blake as he continues to gain in popularity, and I always treasure those moments. Later, I texted him that we hadn't seen him in months and missed him to which he responded, "Guess you need to have another stroke." What can you follow that with other than a wide eyed emoji?

Things had been going badly with Miranda, and on July 6, 2015, Blake filed for divorce. Two weeks later, on July 20, the marriage was over.

Blake was staying busy with *The Voice,* season 9, and ironically future girlfriend, Gwen Stefani, was having similar issues in her own life. She filed for divorce on August 3 of the same year. She was back on the show after being absent in season 8. It was inevitable, or maybe fate, that they opened up to each other first as friends but quickly became more than that. Initially, I thought it was most likely a rebound fling for both of them, but after well over a year, it became obvious that it was much more serious. I have always been a firm believer in *everything happens for a reason.*

On November 15, it was announced that Blake was dating the three-time Grammy Award–winning Gwen Stefani. Gwen, best known as the cofounder and lead vocalist for the American rock band No Doubt has also had success with a solo pop career. Unquestionably multitalented, she is a successful designer and played Jean Harlow in Martin Scorsese's film *The Aviator*, where she received a nomination for a Screen Actors Guild Award.

She is a devoted mom to three young sons Kingston, Zuma, and Apollo Rossdale.

Professionally in 2015, Blake was awarded CMT's Artist of the Year honor for his accomplishments. He also received several award nominations including CMA Male Vocalist and Musical Event: "Lonely Tonight"; People's Choice Favorite Male Artist and Favorite Male Country Artist; and Kids' Choice: Favorite Male Singer. And, he was working hard in the studio with Scott Hendricks on the next album, *If I'm Honest,* squeezing it in between television and a movie.

Blake landed the role of Wyatt Earp in the Adam Sandler movie *The Ridiculous Six,* which was a broad satire of Western movies and the stereotypes they popularized. Maybe I'm prejudiced on this (of course I'm prejudiced on this), but his part was one of the few highlights of the film. It didn't get good reviews and I have to be in agreement on that; however, Netflix reported that it had been seen more times in the first thirty days of its release than any other movie in Netflix's history. You can't argue with success.

Blake isn't a fan of sitting around waiting for a scene and it took Reba McEntire and Lily Tomlin to convince him to be in Reba's situation comedy show *Malibu Country,* playing her younger brother. When Sandler called him personally to offer him the role of Earp in his project, and told him who else would be in it, Blake couldn't say no. However, he lamented that waiting around during a video shoot was nothing compared to a movie, it took two weeks to film his ten-minute scene. It aired in December and prompted me to enroll in Netflix.

American Saturday Night: Live from the Grand Ole Opry also premiered for a limited run in December. It had been filmed by director George J. Flanigen IV in August on location and was the first film shot on that stage. It featured Blake Shelton, Brad Paisley, Darius Rucker, the Band Perry, and Brett Eldredge. Each performed onstage and interacted through interviews backstage. Blake sang "Boys 'Round Here" and "Gonna." The run was extended to select Carmike Cinemas and North American theaters on February 12, 2016.

He also made a cameo appearance in *Pitch Perfect 2* appearing as himself, as judge on *The Voice*. One of the characters in the movie auditioned and Blake was the first to turn his red chair around, but when he saw who it was, he turned the chair back around, something that is never done on the actual show.

Another landmark achievement came when Blake was able to release an album called *Reloaded: 20 #1 Hits*. Imagine that!

With the tough times behind him, Blake told *Country Countdown USA*, "All the awful things that happened in my personal life this year, but the way the year has ended is also the greatest year in my life." When asked for specifics, he added, "I better not talk about that just yet, but sometimes you don't know who's in your life that can save you. I found some people in my life that have changed my life forever. Some has been bad and some that's been pretty good. I'm doing what I'm supposed to do, and that's put all I've gone through into music, and I never felt more connected to a record before. When people hear this record (*If I'm Honest*), they may not know what happened to me, but they're gonna know how I felt about it. And that's exciting for me, to just lay it out there for people."

The first single, "I Came Here to Forget" (Deric Ruttan, Craig Wiseman), from the upcoming album *If I'm Honest*, debuted in March and became his seventeenth #1 in a record-setting string of consecutive hits. It was a good title for his album because Blake is honest to a fault. He might avoid you or not tell you something, but if he says it, you can take it to the bank. I recently ran into Vickie Scott, a teacher from his grade school days at Latta Elementary, and asked her what she remembered about Blake. She said, "I didn't actually teach him and really only remember one thing, that even when he got into trouble, he would always own up to it, tell the truth." What a wonderful quality!

On March 18, Gwen Stefani debuted her third studio album as a solo performer, *This Is What the Truth Feels Like*, documenting her breakup and moving on with a new love. The second single release, "Make Me Like You" (Stefani, Justin Tranter, Julia Michaels, Mattias Larsson, Robin Fredriksson), was inspired by her new relationship with Blake. I know I'm not the only one who became a fan by listening to this album. Coupled with Blake's continuous "You're going to love her!" comments, I couldn't wait to meet Gwen.

I had been anxious for fans to hear the next single, "Savior's Shadow," since first hearing it myself almost a year before. It has an interesting backstory, having come to Blake as a dream in May of the previous year. It was during a time that Oklahoma was having a lot of rain. When he woke up, and before he forgot, he sang the four lines he remembered into his phone. Jessi Alexander and Jon Randall helped him complete the song and interestingly, the final recording was done in his bedroom closet in Los Angeles for perfect acoustics. In an effort to perk me up, he had sent me his original recording of it, along with "Friends," which he had written with Jessi Alexander for the *Angry Birds* movie, while I was still in the hospital the previous year. Pep me up it did! Of course, I immediately knew "Friends" would be nominated for an Oscar. Oh well, it should have been. "Savior's Shadow" was released in April, and was not officially promoted; Blake called gospel radio stations and gave his testimony of how the song came to exist and assured them he was still a country singer and not trying to become more than just that.

The 2016 Country Music Awards proved interesting. Blake was completely snubbed, not one nomination, despite the fact that *If I'm Honest* was the only country music album released that year to sell over five hundred thousand copies and "I Came Here to Forget" became his record-setting seventeenth *consecutive* #1 hit. It made no sense to me. He did win the People's Choice Award for Male Country Artist for the first time after being nominated for five years. He had garnered seven Grammy nominations since 2011 but hadn't taken home a win to date. Another goal maybe?

We got to meet Earl from the *Angry Birds* movie on the big screen May 2016. Blake was the voice for the country-cousin green pig with the lady bugs and barbed wire tattoo in the highly advertised movie inspired by the popular game. As Earl, he only had a few lines, but his country twang added to the movie. He sang the song he and Alexander had written especially for the movie called "Friends," but I don't think those angry birds and their enemies (the green pigs) will ever be friends. The song is catchy and cute. And, when it hit theaters, Larry and I went to see it along with a ton of other Ada kids! It reminded me of the time we went to see the Osmonds years ago when we were vacationing in Nashville without the girls, and everyone except us was about twelve years old. We enjoyed that too! Maybe that is why we have a close bond to Blake; we've never really grown up either.

About that same time, Blake's tenth studio album, *If I'm Honest*, was released, the one with the beautiful cover, a close-up of his face with those blue eyes. I told him that it made me think of my all-time favorite movie star, Paul Newman. He responded with, "That's what I was going for." I feel sure he was being sarcastic, but it is true. It featured fifteen new songs and was again produced by Scott Hendricks, as all of his recordings have been since 2010. Hendricks being another Okie makes you wonder if there really may be something in the water in the great state of Oklahoma.

The following single, "She's Got a Way with Words" (Wyatt Earp, Andy Albert, Marc Beeson), with its satirical lyrics and the timing, easily cracked the top ten but it peaked out at #7, breaking his streak of seventeen consecutive top-ranked songs. In September, he would release "A Guy with a Girl" (Ashley Gorley, Bryan Simpson), featuring Gwen Stefani, as the follow-up to one of my favorite tongue-in-cheek songs ever recorded.

Continuing his philanthropy, Blake donated $600,000 to the Jimmy Everest Center hospital for children with blood cancer and other blood disorders. He held a couple of concerts in Oklahoma City to generate the funds for the donation. His second cousin, Aspen Van Horn, had been treated for cancer at the hospital so there was a personal tie to the cause. He brought little Aspen on stage and shared with his fans her story.

Later, he established the Blake Shelton Cancer Research Program at Oklahoma University's Children's Hospital in honor of Aspen, giving the hospital credit for her success.

Another honor came when Nashville's Country Music Hall of Fame and Museum honored Blake with a special exhibit. Blake Shelton: Based on a True Story ran from May 27–November 6, 2016. On June 7, Blake made an appearance welcoming everyone to the exhibit, which was presented as a time line of his life from childhood to present day. We considered this another major event that we could not miss and made arrangements to be in Nashville and present on that day.

Museum editor Michael McCall moderated a conversation with Blake for an hour, giving him the opportunity to tell his stories that were sprinkled with four songs: "Austin," "Ol' Red," "Sangria," and "She's Got a Way with Words." Blake talked about his first hit, Hoyt Axton introducing him to "Ol' Red," Larry and I moving him to Nashville at age seventeen, Bobby Braddock getting him a label deal and producing him, John Esposito being a great leader and starting the string of #1 hits with "Hillbilly Bone," funny stories about his buddy Trace Adkins and friends from *The Voice*, and finally about his current album, *If I'm Honest*.

It was another memorable day for us. We went from there to the VIP reception where he was introduced by CEO Kyle Young. Blake spoke briefly, welcoming everyone, and then went about visiting with all the friends and business associates in attendance. Bobby Braddock had a cold and wasn't able to make it, but we met up with his daughter, Lauren Braddock Havey, and friends Gayle and Megan Sheehan, and hung around, occasionally meeting someone in the music business that we hadn't known before. I finally got to meet Erin Hay Curtis, whom I had only known through a number of phone calls the past few years. Erin works for Blake's financial manager, Mary Ann McCready, and I felt like I knew her before we actually met. Larry, generally more social than me, was a little miffed that I hadn't found him to give him an introduction to her as well. He was excited to meet William Lee Golden among others, and Brandon Blackstock told us to hang around until everyone left so Blake could visit a little.

We visited and took pictures with Blake for twenty minutes or so and had about five minutes left to experience the exhibit. Even though, by this time in Blake's career, we are lucky to get to see him every few months, it is always like old times. He has a story he remembers and ends up laughing about something. He did take the opportunity to tell us how much we were going to love Gwen. One of the security guards told us to take our time and he would let us out of the building himself, so we were able to really enjoy it. While we were waiting, he had kept pushing us out of the aisle to make room for Blake to come through. When Blake stopped to visit, and probably Brandon told him we were close friends, I think he felt badly. We thought he was doing a good job and told him as much!

The next day Blake called to see if we had plans for that night. He was headlining the twelfth Annual Stars for Second Harvest benefit concert at the Ryman Auditorium along with songwriter and host Craig Wiseman. Wiseman, a prolific songwriter, had penned Blake's #1 hits "Came Here to Forget" and "Boys 'Round Here." We were excited to go and it was a fun evening, with lots of joking around onstage as Wiseman continued to become more inebriated.

The following night we were among Blake's guests at the CMT Music Awards show. Blake won the Social Superstar Award, probably for his infamous tweets on Twitter more than anything else.

He was hilarious when he was doing those on a regular basis. His performance that night was with the Oak Ridge Boys, and he kicked it off with "Doing It to Country Songs" (Jacob Lyda, Paul Overstreet, Marty Dodson), but quickly segued into "Elvira" (Dallas Frazier), which he turned over to the Oaks. You could tell they loved performing their signature song from 1981, and so did the audience. It was a highlight of the evening.

Blake was excited about the next tour and in a press release that announced his early tour dates said, "Man, I'm just so excited about 2016. We've got a new album coming and I can't wait to get back out on the road and play some new music for my fans. As an artist, my favorite thing to do is go on the road and play shows. I've missed it, and it's gonna be like old times. So y'all get ready to party, 'cause Blake Shelton is comin' to see ya!"

It has always been interesting to know what different celebrities put in their contract riders for special foods, and so forth, for their dressing room. We've all heard about an artist wanting just blue M&Ms, that sort of thing. So, in case you are wondering what Blake's needs are, look no further than thesmokinggun.com, which reports the following information: "Shelton's alcohol demands are notable only for their moderation. His rider asked for two cases of light, canned beer and two bottles apiece of Bacardi Clear Rum and Cabernet Sauvignon. The singer also requires a four-pack of that horrendous 5-Hour energy drink you see advertised on basic cable, as well as a dozen cans of sugar-free Red Bull. All beverages are to be delivered to Shelton's tour bus, which apparently has a spacious refrigerator. After a concert, promotion personnel must make another trip to Shelton's brown/black ride to deliver two grilled chicken salads and fat free Ranch and Italian dressing. And, of course, one large Pizza Hut Meat Lovers or Stuffed Crust Supreme pizza."

Gwen was also busy touring July–October promoting *This Is What the Truth Feels Like* in the United States and Canada. Her album was also an outlet for her following her divorce. When she had a free weekend, she would often join Blake on his tour as well.

Once again, Blake made arrangements for us to go out with him on a long weekend run in September. RaeLynn, who had been a contestant on *The Voice* in season 2, was the opening act for the Doin' It to Country Music tour. We would have the opportunity for some long visits that time. He was in Los Angeles and we were in Ada, so he had his bus drive to Ardmore to pick us up and drive to Wichita to meet him when he flew there from L.A. It was just us and Kevin with Blake on the bus and we always have a good time with them both. We usually relive old times and that is always good for a laugh; there is nothing like a "remember that time we . . ." and everyone just starts laughing without having to actually repeat the entire story, though someone usually does. There are a kazillion of those stories. He usually has some secret to share that we can't tell anyone, usually pretty easy for me, not so easy for Larry. This time, it was about some ideas he had to help business in downtown Tishomingo.

He told us all about the new place that was finally finished at Lake Texoma. We had driven down there when it was being built but hadn't done that since its completion. We were planning a trip to Myrtle Beach with some friends (a hurricane later wiped out those plans), but Blake was telling us that his house would be more fun. Kevin agreed and even offered to pay our deposit to cancel our plans if we would go check it out. Of course, we couldn't let him do that, but it just goes to show what good people Blake has on his team now and how they have also accepted us as their friends. We love Kevin too!

Gwen Stefani had been out with him the past two weeks but didn't come out that particular weekend. I kept teasing Blake, as I had done for months, that he was afraid for me to meet her. Gwen had been coming out toward the end of Blake's shows and singing a song and the crowd absolutely loved her. So the weekend we went, she wasn't there, but it was easy enough to see that Blake missed her. I had taken him a leather engraved Bible and a book of daily devotionals that a fan had sent him. They were beautiful and his first comment was, "Gwen will love reading this."

"Go Ahead and Break My Heart," written and performed as a duet by Blake and Gwen Stefani, was released in September as a promotional single. They first performed it on season 10 of *The Voice*. Both of them have huge fan bases and everyone loved their first effort as a duo. Blake said that when they first started dating, they were both having some serious insecurities and trust issues. They were getting over it, but in the process, this song came along. Blake wrote the first verse and sent it to her. She wrote the next verse and before long they had a perfect song. It gives people a glimpse into their early days together when they were both expecting to possibly get their hearts broken again. They loved singing it at shows and I'm sorry we missed a live performance of it.

During our time that long weekend, we hung around backstage a lot talking to people. Blake was doing a new VIP experience that I hadn't seen before so I went to it. He did a little question/answer session and sang a few songs to about fifty people. There was a photo booth and a couple of other photo opportunities, one being a bigger than life-size paper cutout of Blake, and there was a bar. A nice guy from Warner Bros. took us around and kept us from getting lost. Blake had a new assistant, a girl from Tishomingo, who was beyond helpful and kept asking if we needed anything. But what we like most when we aren't visiting with Blake or Kevin is just wandering around. There is usually a back-lot basketball game and Larry loves to visit with all the guys, especially those that were with Blake thirteen years ago when he was last on the road full-time. It didn't take him long to get to know the newer guys too, though. Blake has a great band: Rob Byus (bass guitar), Tracy Broussard (drums), Beau Tackett (lead guitar), Phillip de Steiguer (keyboard), Jenee Fleenor (fiddle), Kevin Post (guitar/steel guitar), and Kara Britz (vocalist).

Of course, I always go to sound check and often request "Shame Shame Shame" (Mark Collie, Jackson Lee Leap), the Mark Collie song Blake used to sing at the McSwain. It was my favorite from that time frame. I don't know that Blake has ever actually taken the request, but he knows I like it. He remembers the smallest things, like my favorite word, "onomatopoeia." I guarantee you could ask him, "What is Carol's favorite word?" and he wouldn't blink before he responded with the correct answer.

Blake's good friend Tom McMillan (who has a show on the Sportsman Channel) came to the Wichita show along with wife Jacque and son Gattlin. Three-year-old Gattlin was the biggest little gentleman I've ever met. He shook hands with everyone along with "Pleased to meet you" and a big smile. I had met Tom and Jacque before and was happy to see them again.

After the show, we all went to a room backstage so there was room for everyone to visit. There I became mesmerized by Jazz, RaeLynn's service dog. I learned that RaeLynn has type 1 diabetes and her service dog Jazz is her constant companion. He was totally dedicated to her, never leaving her side. She told a story of how he woke her one morning by pushing the curtain to her bunk aside and licking her face. He wouldn't leave her alone until she got up and checked her blood sugar, which was dangerously low, and she was able to correct it. I was full of questions after that and couldn't take my eyes off the amazing dog that guarded the tiny performer.

By 2:00 a.m., we were headed to Fargo, North Dakota. After visiting just a little, we all crawled into our bunks and woke up there the next day. I can see how the road gets a little boring for the guys and gals who do it for a living, but we never get bored on our one weekend a year.

The next morning, Blake and I were sitting at a little booth-type table on the bus as he sipped coffee and we were looking out the window. Larry had already gone to breakfast. RaeLynn was crawling off her bus with her dog. Blake was smiling when he said, "I just love her." I love those early mornings too, when the world is waking up and you see into people's routines, but I am a night person and usually sleep through that part of the day unless I'm on vacation.

We visited a while and Blake got ready for his busy schedule. There is so much more than simply getting to a venue, singing ninety minutes, and leaving. The routine for us was also about the same but we do enjoy meeting the workers at the venues and in one day, they know who we are and we know their names—temporarily.

That evening, Blake asked us if we wanted to follow him through the tunnel that led to the elevator under the stage that enabled him to make an entrance up through the stage floor. Well of course we did! He had to duck to go through the lengthy path with a tent-type cover and when we got to the end, he stepped into the elevator and we slipped out a little door with a Velcro fastener and onto the side of the stage where again we watched the entire show. The only variation from that routine was one night we made sure to catch RaeLynn's performance. There's a bundle of talent tied up in that small package!

After the show, RaeLynn and some of the girls travelling with her came to the bus and they sang a little. She is a songwriter as well as a singer and many of her songs have some creatively funny lyrics. I thoroughly enjoyed sitting there watching them joke around and sing. It was easy to see why Blake enjoys her; they have the same crazy and sometimes uncensored sense of humor. They make fun of each other in much the same way as Blake and Endy; he considers her like a younger sister.

Early on, during our time on the bus, I told Blake that I had been teasing Debi and Patti that I was going to try smoking pot. I told them I had seen Reba on Andy Cohen's show where she talked about trying it and I figured that if she could, so could I, and had been repeating that sentiment incessantly, adding that when I got the chance, I was going to do it. I had kind of forgotten about telling Blake that story.

One evening at catering, I had a salad and knew I would finish before the guys so had picked up a little paper bowl and filled it with an odd assortment of munchables: a baby carrot, a handful of eight peanut M&Ms, three olives, three tortilla chips, and a small wedge of watermelon to nibble on while they finished. I didn't even see Blake take a picture of it with his cell phone, and Patti still has it.

Later, on the bus, we were sitting around and he was looking at his phone laughing. I asked what was so funny and he handed me his phone. He had sent Patti the picture and she had responded:

Patti: What the heck is that? Worst lunch ever.

Blake: Your mom, not kidding.

Patti: That's literally awful; it looks like what a three-year-old would serve to their parent.

Blake: Ha, she's probably high!

Patti: I blame Reba!

Blake lost it!

We woke up the next day in Sioux Falls, South Dakota. That morning, I told Blake that in case it got hectic and I didn't get a chance to tell him how much fun we had, I wanted him to know and that I realize we are a bit of a pain in the butt, but that we have more fun than we care about that. He laughed and said that we really weren't, that we just get out and do our own thing and that he doesn't have to worry with making sure we are entertained. I don't know if that is the truth or not, but he made me believe it. It is simply the best time to get to know his frame of mind and this trip showed us that he is happier than he has ever been. Blake is a good person, loyal to a fault until someone breaks that bond, and I couldn't be happier that he is happy with his life. That is the same morning I told him that I just might write a book about our times with him and he told me, "Go for it!"

After the show, the bus took us to the airport where we boarded his private jet and took off for Oklahoma. Rob Byus (bass player/

friend) and Joel Borski (husband of stylist Amanda Craig Borski/ friend) joined Blake, Kevin, and us back to Ardmore, Oklahoma, where we had our car waiting and they had a helicopter take them to Blake's lodge for an upcoming hunting trip. They had worked hard for four straight days and were now ready for some fun. We had fun for four straight days and were now ready for some rest.

A unique event occurred when thirty country music artists, including Blake, calling themselves Then, Now and Forever, videoed and recorded "Forever Country," a mashup of three previous hits: "Take Me Home Country Roads" (Bill Danoff, Taffy Nivert, John Denver), "On the Road Again" (Willie Nelson), and "I Will Always Love You" (Dolly Parton) to commemorate the CMA Awards' fiftieth year. The video was directed by Joseph Kahn and the song was recorded over a three-day period in Nashville with Shane McAnally producing. Profits from the sale and streaming of the song would go to music education supported by the CMA Foundation. It debuted #1 on *Billboard*'s Hot Country Songs chart and gave every artist featured a #1 hit!

In October, Gwen, who is part Italian, was asked to perform at the White House at a state dinner honoring Italian prime minister Matteo Renzi and his wife Agnese Landini. Blake attended along with her and her children, giving me only one degree of separation from the president of the United States. My bucket is getting empty; I'm going to have to make a new list.

It wasn't for another few months that I finally got to meet Blake's love Gwen Stefani during the Christmas break. We didn't have a long time to visit but what a great first impression! We had gone to Dorothy's to drop off some Christmas gifts and as we were leaving, I got a text from Blake asking if we were in town, so we stopped by to see them. They were getting ready to cook sausage balls for a family dinner later.

As 2016 wound down, *Billboard* used data from the last fifty years to create "Greatest of All Time Country Artists." Blake came in at #50. He also came in at #80 in the songs list for "God Gave Me You" and #51 in albums list for *Based on a True Story*. In addition, the American Music Awards presented him the award for Favorite Country Male Artist of the Year.

In my never-ending efforts to try to get Blake more interested in reading, I gave him two books of O. Henry stories for Christmas that year. They are so much like songs that I thought there might be a chance. I know that Blake much prefers listening to reading, but I am a lover of books and an optimist!

CHAPTER TEN

YOU CAN'T MAKE THIS UP

At a January 5, 2017, press conference, Blake made it known that he had joined forces with Ryman Hospitality Properties, Inc. to create a $20 million multilevel entertainment venue on Lower Broadway in Nashville, Tennessee, set to open in April 2018. Combining the names of Blake's signature song, "Ol' Red" with the Grand Ole Opry, it would be known as "Ole Red." In making the announcement, Colin Reed (chairman and CEO of RHP) proclaimed, "The Grand Ole Opry is known for connecting fans to the artists and the music they love and that is what the Ole Red brand is all about. Not only is Blake Shelton one of the most popular entertainers of his generation, his performance style and passion for authentic country music have also made him a fixture on the Grand Ole Opry stage since the early days of his career. Ole Red will immerse fans in all the elements of a great country song with some unexpected twists from Blake along the way."

The Nashville site would feature a five-story bar and restaurant as well as retail and performance spaces. Also featured would be an indoor/outdoor bar and restaurant atop the roof offering guests a view of the city below. Possibly more exciting for fans was the future Ole Red Tishomingo in Oklahoma, which was scheduled to launch September 2017. Blake felt strongly that he wanted to bring something new to the town he now called home. He said, "It's amazing to me to see a song that's been such a big part of my career come to life in the plans for Ole Red. Nashville and Tishomingo are both places that are important to me and it's great that each location is going to have its own personality inspired by one of my favorite songs. It's always been a dream of mine to create something like this where people know they're going to have a good time as soon as they walk in the door, and I couldn't be more excited that my friends at the Opry and Ryman Hospitality Properties are making it happen." (Ole Red Nashville would open on June 7, 2018, following the opening of Ole Red Tishomingo on September 30, 2017.)

Also in January, "A Guy with a Girl" (Ashley Gorley, Bryan Simpson), the fourth single from *If I'm Honest,* became Blake's twenty-third career #1, putting him right back atop the charts! In a press release, Blake said, "I've been in this business long enough to know that a #1 single should be celebrated and never taken for granted. I'm just as excited about 'Guy with a Girl' going #1 as I was with 'Austin.' The first thing I did when I found out today was call my mom, just like I did with my first and every #1. So, as always, thanks to country radio and especially the fans for this."

Fans were excited that Blake was asked to perform at the People's Choice Awards on January 18, and debut the new single "Every Time I Hear That Song" (Aimee Mayo, Chris Lindsey, Brad Warren, Brett Warren). At that show, he took home the win for Favorite Male Country Artist for the second year in a row. The big surprise was his win for Album of the Year: *If I'm Honest,* an all-genre award. It marked the first time ever a country artist had taken home the Favorite Album prize. In his acceptance speech for both awards, which followed his performance, he imagined people were asking themselves how it happened that he could win the top album award because "Isn't it just a country album full of stereotypical country songs?" Blake adamantly responded to the viewers with, "You're damn right it is!" He was also nominated for Favorite Male Artist, another all-genre category, but lost to the talented and popular Justin Timberlake; still, it was a huge honor to be considered in that category. Breaking into the all-genre categories is a big deal. Blake is proud to take country there! He was also nominated for Best Lyrics: "I Came Here to Forget" at the iHeart Radio awards; the winner was Justin Bieber: "Love Yourself" (Ed Sheeran, Benjamin Levin, Bieber).

There was no slowing down for Blake in January. He joined Luke Bryan at his Crash My Playa event in Mexico. Also on the show was Little Big Town, who talked about the experience with *Country Countdown USA*'s Lon Helton. They said the most fun were some impromptu jam sessions of singing old country songs on the beach 'til two in the morning. They also did some on the Saturday night show. Karen Fairchild (LBT member) said, "I've never met anybody that knows more songs than Blake. He's like a human juke box."

Luke Bryan said that Blake pulled out songs he hadn't thought of in fifteen or twenty years, and he knew every word. Bryan added, "I figured he wouldn't know the second verse, but he knew every song from top to bottom." They did that for several nights. And, a special bonus was when Blake called Gwen Stefani out to join him on "Footloose" (Kenny Loggins, Dean Pitchford), and then continue with some of her big hits. Blake joked that Luke wouldn't be able to afford what she was going to charge. It sounded like they had a lot of fun.

In February, "Every Time I Hear That Song" (Aimee Mayo, Chris Lindsey, Brad Warren, Bret Warren) was released and Blake commenced his Doing It to Country Songs tour in Bakersfield, California. RaeLynn and Sundance Head, recent Team Blake winner from *The Voice*, would join him on the tour. The name of the tour was inspired by a track on Blake's tenth studio album, *If I'm Honest*. As the tour got under way, Blake said, "Performing for an audience is what I love most, and if you're coming to see me, you're coming to hear country music, because that's what I do."

Blake has supported his team members after their stints on *The Voice* are over. He encouraged Universal Records to give their full support as well to Sundance Head, the 2016 winner from Blake's team.

An interesting event occurred in March. Nashville brought Blake back to Music City in the form of a wax figure, which was unveiled at Madame Tussauds. It didn't get a great deal of publicity, but I have always been mesmerized by wax museums. I can't believe I still haven't been down there to see it; I'm not even sure it is still there.

April 3 was another big day for Blake in Oklahoma as he was in Tishomingo to drive the first nail in the Ole Red building. The hope is that the business mascot, Ol' Red, will be tracking customers all over the United States in the near future. While Tishomingo will hold the honor of being the first Ole Red's, the Nashville location would be only months behind it, hopefully with more to come in major cities across America. (Ole Red Gatlinburg would quickly follow, opening on March 13, 2019. The pandemic delayed Ole Red Orlando from opening on June 19, 2020, but it would finally open almost a year later on April 15, 2021. Plans were already underway for an Ole Red Airport in Nashville in 2022.) And to polish off the day, he was honored as one of the 2017 Oklahoma Creativity Ambassadors, recognizing him as one of the state's most creative leaders.

Over a dozen festival appearances were scheduled for 2017, April–September, and *The Voice* shows went live in mid-April. We attended the finale on May 22–23! He would no sooner wrap that up until they began shooting for the next season. Busy, busy, busy!

And then there is this: paparazzi zinged me and I have to share my unfortunate experience. I realize Blake puts up with these untrue stories all the time and I have always tried to be on my guard. But one pleasant June afternoon, a girl showed up on my front porch asking questions. I knew what she was and should have just shut the door, but Oklahomans are friendly by nature and I am not often rude. I stepped out and spoke with her a few minutes. I made it clear by voicing it several times that I had nothing bad to say about anybody. Do you think Blake and Gwen will marry? I don't know. Do you think if they do you will be invited to the wedding? I would hope so. Did you know Miranda? Yes. Do you think she is different than Gwen? Yes. Did you like Miranda? Yes. Do you think Blake and Gwen will have babies? That's personal and I don't know. You get the picture.

The article came out in one of the most famous of the sensational yellow rags with my interview. It included a twenty-three-year-old photograph of me and Blake that they must have taken from Facebook without permission and cropped out my husband. (He was smarter than me; he wouldn't talk to the girl.) I haven't bought any of that genre of print media since Princess Diana died during a paparazzi chase over twenty years ago. Most people know the stories are generally bogus. Once in a while, they have something that turns out to be true and it convinces some people that they might be getting a scoop. There's been a lot of talk lately about fake news. This is the perfect example of fake news, just dreaming up stuff or taking things out of context to make people want to read it. I miss the days of the aliens living among us or the 134-year-old woman giving birth to twins. Just saying, don't believe what you read about celebrities. They are just like you and me, only more well-known. Don't buy it!

But the part that really still annoys me is the way people react. A friend of Larry's for more than fifty years called him and said, "What's this I hear about Carol talking bad about Blake?" Larry responded, "Have you ever heard Carol say anything bad about Blake?" Silence and then, "No, but it said in this magazine." Frustrated by the conversation, Larry said, "You can't believe that crap in those magazines . . . who are you going to believe . . . your friend or a magazine?" Silence.

In July, "Every Time I Hear That Song" scored Blake's twenty-fourth career #1!

Gwen Stefani released "You Make It Feel Like Christmas" (Stefani, Justin Tranter, Shelton, Busbee) from her album of the same name in September. Blake was a featured singer on the song and in the holiday special, *Gwen Stefani's You Make It Feel Like Christmas.*

In mid-October, Blake invited us to use his lake house for a week. We took couple friends, Farrell and Sue Large and Gil and Barbara

Ragland. We just messed around, went out on the boat, drove the golf cart all over, swam, spent time in the spa area, visited, waved at boaters—just a great time! We watched *The Voice* from there and sent Blake a selfie of us in front of his television. Fun!

"I'll Name the Dogs" (Josh Thompson, Ben Hayslip, Matt Dragstrem) was released as the lead-off single from Blake's eleventh studio album, *Texoma Shore*, which would be released on November 3.

And then, on November 14, Blake made the cover of *People* magazine as 2017's "Sexiest Man Alive." His response was, "I can't wait to shove this up Adam's ass!" Having had that honor in 2013, Adam never thought in a million years that he would get paid back for all the jokes he poked at Blake. (Remember the huge cut out of the magazine's cover he had delivered to Blake in Oklahoma!) Actually, it was a cool thing; Blake and Adam have been the only musicians to receive that honor. In fact, they won the MTV Movie and TV Award as 2017's Best Duo. And, on his fourth nomination, Blake was named *Billboard*'s Top Country Artist of 2017.

On January 29, 2018, "I Lived It" (Rhett Akins, Ashley Gorley, Ben Hayslip, Ross Copperman) was released as the second single from *Texoma Shore*, peaking at #3 on *Billboard*'s Country Airplay.

Continuing to give back, Blake took his Country Music Freaks spring tour to Tishomingo on February 9 and 10, where all proceeds were donated to charity. The fourteen-date tour officially kicked off the following week in Tulsa, featuring Brett Eldridge and Carly Pearce, in addition to special guest Trace Adkins. It was a great concert! Endy took one of my favorite pictures of me at that show.

Blake sent a bus for us and we joined him in March for a weekend run beginning in Houston at the rodeo. His producer, Scott Hendricks, was also traveling with him, so I finally did get to visit with him a little. Through the years, Scott has produced seventy-five #1 hits and tons of top 10s. He is currently Warner Music Nashville's executive vice president of A&R. By the time we joined Blake, he was already not feeling well. He had a fever and thought he had the flu. He was taking medicine and trying to get over it, hoping he could finish the weekend before going home for rest and recovery. The performance on March 1 at the Houston Rodeo went off well. I don't think anyone would have known he was battling the flu if he hadn't told them.

From there we went to Dallas, Texas, where he continued to feel worse, and that night I could tell he did not feel like being onstage. Attempting to power through, we persevered on to Bossier City, Louisiana. When we got there, Blake saw a doctor (coincidentally, he told me she was really a gynecologist? Maybe joking), who told him to cancel the show and get well, that it was not healthy to do the show and he could possibly do permanent damage to his voice. I was in the venue watching them set up, and they were well on their way, when an announcement came over the intercom to tear it down; the show was being postponed. Blake realizes his fans sometimes travel great distances and make complicated arrangements to see him and he hated to postpone the show, but there was really no choice. As soon as we could, the buses pulled out and we headed home. I was concerned that Blake had pushed himself too far, but he recovered and did the show at a later date.

Meanwhile, the third single from *Texoma Shore*, "Turnin' Me On" (Shelton, Josh Osborne, Jessi Alexander) was released on July 30 and peaked at #10 on the *Billboard* Hot Country Airplay chart.

Those awards I always thought Blake deserved came pretty steadily throughout this entire decade. Blake had seventeen nominations for the *Teen Choice Awards* (2011–2018), twenty-seven awards from the *BMI Country Awards* (2011–2019), and twenty-seven country music awards from *ASCAP* (2002–2019). September 19 featured the inaugural of the Nashville Songwriter Awards at the famed Ryman Auditorium, and Blake's song "I'll Name the Dogs" (Matt Dragstrem, Ben Hayslip, Josh Thompson) took top honors as Song of the Year. He also won the Country Artist Award at the People's Choice Awards. Being fan generated, the People's Choice Awards are always a little special. Blake was honored with the Artist Humanitarian Award for his benevolent work over the course of 2018, on February 13, 2019, during day one of the Country Radio Seminar.

His 2019 Friends and Heroes tour kicked off the next day in Oklahoma City on February 14, and ran through March 23. It featured the Bellamy Brothers, John Anderson, Trace Adkins, and Lauren Alaina.

The grand opening of Ole Red Gatlinburg (Tennessee) on March 13, 2019, earned $29,214. That, along with $25,000 from Ryman Hospitality Properties was donated to Gatlinburg-Pittman High School's music programs.

We took another short vacation to Blake's lake house at Lake Texoma in mid-May. We had started what we hoped would become a tradition of going in spring and fall when most friends/family weren't that interested in the lake. It is just a great place to unwind and get away to a happy place that feels very tropical. He has the yard adorned with eighteen palm trees, something you don't see often in Oklahoma. We just always have a fabulous time there.

In July, we cashed in our American Express points and flew to Vegas to catch Gwen's exclusive headlining residency show, *Gwen Stefani: Just a Girl*, in Zappos Theater at Planet Hollywood Resort and Casino. Gwen is a three-time Grammy Award winner who has sold more than thirty million albums worldwide with her band No Doubt and as a solo artist. She is also an accomplished fashion designer, having created the popular brand L.A.M.B. I was somewhat familiar with her and her band but it was all completely new to Larry. As we exited that night, Larry said, "Well, I get it now!" and I heard him say that a few more times as he shouted her praises to his friends. The show was two hours of pure energy. She never slowed down; even costume changes seemed to take place in less than a minute. It was a thrill when she recognized us from the audience and told a little of our connection to Blake. But the part of the evening we loved most was meeting backstage with her for about thirty minutes before the show. It was just us and

Gwen and she was very open, sharing things I know she doesn't share with everyone and I would never break the confidence she must have felt by opening up like she did. She did say that Blake had told her a lot about us. Everyone who had spent time with her had complimented her as a great human being and we had met her a couple of times before and felt she was super nice. But this one-on-one visit secured a spot in my heart for Gwen Stefani. She holds up to the kajillion times I had heard Blake say, "She's great; you're gonna love her!"

From Vegas, we flew to Reno, Nevada, to spend a couple of days with Larry's cousin Byron Auten, his wife Louise, and their grand-daughter Bobbie, and to take in Blake's concert at Lake Tahoe before flying home to Oklahoma. We also met up with my California cousins, Sharon and Ron Stone and Mae and Bruce Gribbin. I was so happy to meet them, especially Bruce, as he suddenly passed less than a week later. We squeezed a lot into just four days but it was worth it!

August 7 turned out to be a special day for us. Blake called about noon and asked what we were doing. I responded with something like, "We live in Ada." He said, "Well, be at the airport at 3:00; I'll have you home by bedtime." When we got there, it was just him and his mom, Dorothy, on the plane and I didn't even ask where we were going. Turned out, he was having a #1 party for "God's Country" that evening at the Nashville Ole Red bar and restaurant. His manager Narvel Blackstock picked us up and we squeezed into his car. He took the long route, since we hadn't been in Nashville for three years and he wanted to show us how much it had changed. It was unbelievable! We finally wound up at Ole Red and went in the back way to the waiting room. While we were in there, Larry was visiting with Dorothy and pointed to a picture of Johnny and June Carter Cash leaving Folsom Prison and said, "Wouldn't you love to have that picture?" He didn't think any more about it, but Dorothy got a copy of the photograph and framed it for him for Christmas. He was both shocked and pleased that she remembered.

Anyway, back to the party, it was packed to the brim and hot so I just stayed long enough for the main introductions and to hear Blake and the songwriters (Devin Dawson, Jordan Schmidt, Hardy) each have something to say, and then I went back across the hall to the waiting room where it was cooler. Narvel asked if we had tried the pretzels, that they were amazing. We hadn't, so he went to get us some. They are huge and delicious, so if you're ever there, try one. While everyone was visiting, someone came across and told me Blake said someone was asking about me. It was one of the songwriters' moms wanting to meet me! Ha! It turned out that she is a hair stylist and one of her patrons is my former principal from Hillsboro Elementary Middle School in Leiper's Fork, Ann Lewis. She was styling Ann's hair and telling her about her son's #1 party and when Blake's name came up, Ann told her about me and Larry. It is such a small world!

Sadly, Blake's friend Earl Thomas Conley, passed on April 10, 2019. Earl did not want a funeral, but his wife Carole Scates, decided to honor his memory with a special concert at the CMA Theater at Nashville's Country Music Hall of Fame and Museum. We had emailed each other back and forth a few times regarding charity events and such, so she wrote to ask if I thought Blake would be interested in participating in the concert. I knew he would if he could and they worked it out. Earl Thomas Conley: A Tribute Celebration of Life and Music took place on September 10, 2019. Blake, along with Jason Aldean, John Anderson, Luke Bryan, Joe Diffie, Wade Hayes, Neal McCoy, bluegrass instrumentalist Dale Ann Bradley, Conley's daughter Erinn Scates, and the Earl Thomas Conley Band performed. Conley had eighteen #1 singles and had been Blake's favorite artist since he was ten years old, when he saw him in a commercial and noticed how much emotion was in his voice and that he had "sad eyebrows." He knew immediately that he wanted to sing Earl's 1988 hit, "What I'd Say" (Robert Byrne, Will Robinson).

Carole invited us and our travel buddies (Gil, Barbara, Farrell, and Sue) to the memorial. We flew to Nashville on the ninth and stayed through the thirteenth so we could check out all the changes in downtown since we had last been there. We met our friends Patty and Warren Kerckhoff for breakfast one morning and had a nice visit with them. We took in all the bars and even a jazz club one night. We also went to the museum and branched off and did other stuff on our own. We travel together, but we aren't joined at the hip. We all had a good time reliving old memories that week.

Being a man of many talents, on October 12, Blake officiated the wedding of Trace Adkins and Canadian actress Victoria Pratt in New Orleans, Louisiana. People are always surprised he does that, but I know of at least three weddings he has officiated.

Speaking of weddings, Larry and I had a big anniversary coming up in November and we had talked to Blake a little about it on the flight to Nashville. He kind of felt us out on what we wanted and was talking to Debi and Patti about it. We change our minds often, so it wasn't easy to plan. It would have probably been easier on them had it been a surprise, but we got to be part of the planning. Blake set it up for us to use the Doghouse (performance venue) at Ole Red/Tishomingo and his townhouse across the street for us and our closest friends. Dorothy opened her townhouse next door to some of my out-of-town cousins. And a couple of nearby motels and bed and breakfasts housed the rest of those who came long distances. We had friends and family from six or seven states in attendance and a bunch of friends from Ada. We pretty much filled the place. We hired Telina Rudd and the Red Clay Gypsies, because she is a great entertainer and performs cover songs from Bruno Mars to Michael Jackson to George Jones and everyone in between. We had so many different age groups in attendance that we wanted to offer something for everyone, and she fit the bill. She even sang *our* song, Paul Anka's "Put Your Head on My Shoulder." Everyone loved her. Patti had set it up ahead of time with the band for Megan Sheehan to sing a surprise song for us. I guess they knew what it was, but we didn't until that night. She sang, "You Belong to Me" (Chilton Price, PeeWee King, Redd Stewart) and it was perfect. Even Larry got up to play drums and sing a little that night, as did guitarist/singer Alan Rudd. Lots of coincidences with Alan: he is Telina's dad; we taught with him in both Konawa, Oklahoma, and Leiper's Fork, Tennessee; and he participated in the band jams that they had periodically. He also has a great voice.

Everyone ate, drank, and was merry for the evening. It is the best party I've ever had and everyone had a great time. I had even talked to Blake about having it become an annual event. The party was on the eighth but we stayed November 7–10 and got to know Tishomingo very well.

During 2019, Blake had released "God's Country" March 29, and it went #1 on Hot Country Songs by mid-year. Then "Hell Right" (David Garcia, Hardy, Brett Tyler), another duet with Trace Adkins, was released August 16, peaking at #14 on Hot Country Songs. Both of those singles came from his fifth compilation album, *Fully Loaded: God's Country*, which debuted at #1 on *Billboard*'s Top Country Albums on December 13.

"God's Country" brought Blake a win for CMA's Single of the Year, as well as a nomination for Music Video of the Year. He and Garth were nominated for Musical Event of the Year for "Dive Bar." And I can't leave out his fiddle player/friend Jenee Fleenor, who broke the glass ceiling as the first female to be nominated for Musician of the Year. Oh, and she won it too! That year, Blake was also nominated for Favorite Country Song at the *ACM Awards*.

Billboard released decade rankings and Blake did pretty well. For Top Country Albums: *Based on a True Story* was #14, while *Reloaded: 20 #1 Hits* came in at #24, *If I'm Honest* #49, and *Red River Blue* #50. In the Top Country Songs: "God Gave Me You" #19, "Honey Bee" #23, and "God's Country" #26. For Top *Billboard* 200 Albums: *Based on a True Story* #51.

Blake ended 2019 on the Hot Country Songs chart with fifty-two entries, the most of any country artist this decade!

CHAPTER ELEVEN

GOD'S COUNTRY

"**N**obody But You" (Ross Copperman, Shane McAnally, Josh Osborne, Tommy Lee James), (not to be confused with "Nobody But Me" from the *Blake Shelton's Barn and Grill* album a few years earlier) a duet with Gwen, was the third single released from the *Fully Loaded: God's Country* album on January 21, 2020. The single went to #1 on the Digital Songs chart as well as *Billboard's* Country Airplay US and Canada, and peaked at #18 on the *Billboard* Hot 100. Blake and Gwen have performed the song several times, including at the 62nd Annual Grammy Awards (where Blake also received his ninth nomination for a Grammy, this time for Best Country Solo Performance, "God's Country") and as a surprise during Gwen's residency in Las Vegas. The video, directed by Sophie Muller, gives fans a glimpse into their life with scenes from their day-to-day activities in Oklahoma.

We had missed the Friends and Heroes tour in 2019, but Blake suggested we come out for the weekend of February 20–22 for the Bakersfield/Fresno/Sacramento leg of the tour. He said if we could get to Bakersfield, he would get us home. So we booked a one-way flight and off we went. When we got there, a driver picked us up at the airport and took us to the bus. We were excited to see everyone again and it turned out that Gwen would be there the next day, so we were anxious to see her too. The show was great. Lauren Alaina has an amazing voice and we loved seeing her each night. We had a great lunch one day with John Anderson. I told him that I thought I remembered that he had worked on the roof of the Grand Ole Opry building before he made it big with "Swingin'" (John Anderson, Lionel Delmore) and asked him if my memory was correct. He confirmed that bit of trivia that I had tucked away somewhere in my overcrowded brain. He talked about fishing and all kinds of stuff. When we got up to have a picture made together, we realized that we were all three dressed similarly (denim head to toe) and kind of looked like a singing group from the 1970s. It was a nice experience meeting and chatting for a lengthy amount of time with a guy we had heard on radio for years. He was very nice.

The next day, we met up with Gwen and Blake where he was playing basketball in back of the venue and she was visiting with Lauren. It was that weekend that I met Gwen's brother Todd Stefani, who travels with Blake and videos him for social networking. In fact, he asked if he could join us on our bus as we were less crowded and we loved getting to know him. He is the one who introduced me to intermittent fasting and I think it is the best diet for me that I've ever found.

I think it was the last night, Blake came on the bus with a recorder. He wanted to record some stories. Larry was already in bed but we sat and relived old times for a couple of hours, just the two of us. It was neat because Larry and I constantly interrupt each other when we are together. Blake and I laughed and relived some old times at the Music Palace and the McSwain.

All three shows had been fabulous. We either sat with Pig at the soundboard or offstage. I was surprised to see William Shatner at the Fresno concert. I was a huge fan of *Boston Legal*. I'm so happy that we had that weekend because he'd only done one or two more stints when everything shut down, probably for a good while. Endy and Mike didn't get to go out as planned. It was disappointing to them as well as the many fans. So I feel extremely lucky that we had that opportunity.

After the last show, we flew back to Oklahoma with Blake and they dropped us off at Will Rogers World Airport in Oklahoma City, where we had left our car a few days earlier.

On Friday, the 13th of March, Gil and Barbara asked us to go with them to Purcell and eat at Jo's Famous Pizza. COVID-19 was already starting to spread across the nation, but it hadn't hit

Oklahoma much. Still, I carried Clorox wipes and hand disinfectant (though I had been carrying little Bath & Body hand sanitizers for years), and when I wiped down the table, the waitress looked at me and told me she had cleaned the tables. I told her to not pay any attention to me, that I am a bit of a germophobe. Anyway, the food was delicious and so good that the last time eating out was a pleasant memory. We had decided we would go back, and we will some day. But beginning Saturday, March 14, 2020, we began self-isolation. Speaking of eating out, Larry and I ate out *every* day before the quarantine and though I also have a major in home economics (cooking and sewing), I never learned the love of cooking. I laughingly admit that I have the taste buds of a twelve-year-old who doesn't like meat. (After the full year we spent in quarantine with my cooking, I don't care if I ever cook again.)

Meanwhile in April, Blake donated $150,000 to the Give from Home Day fundraiser, a partnership between Oklahoma City's affiliate KOCO-5 and the Regional Food Bank of Oklahoma with the goal of helping feed the hungry during the COVID-19 pandemic. During parts of March and April, his merchandise was reduced in price and a portion of sales was donated to Music-Cares, COVID-19's relief fund.

Along with most television shows that were still airing, The *Voice* continued with both contestants and judges doing their jobs from home. On May 11, they were filming the final performances. Larry and I drove to Tishomingo, where Blake and Todd were filming his part and met up with them face to face. We still stayed distant but they were the first live faces I'd seen in two months, except Larry and Lily and Margie, our mini-poodles. We had all been staying to ourselves, so felt pretty safe. The next night, we watched live on television when forty-two-year-old Todd Tighman was named the eighteenth season *Voice* winner, giving Coach Blake Shelton his seventh victory!

Larry went out to pick up groceries I had ordered using Walmart's online shopping because he could pick up there without having to touch anything. When he got home, I disinfected everything, including doorknobs and light switches that he touched after bringing in the groceries. Occasionally he got stir crazy and sneaked out to our neighborhood grocery, Dicus Supermarket, and assured me they had safety precautions as well. But whenever he brought anything home, I wiped it down. It was a crazy time!

Our daughter Debi lives in Ada and we usually take a drive on Sunday afternoon, so we had been stopping at her house and staying in the car to visit with her in her back yard. But she had been working from home and being cautious too, so I finally got comfortable with going over there some. Even Patti drove from Texas one day and we distance visited but at least got to see her. She didn't even sit at the table with us, but at a TV tray across the room. And our living room is long so she stayed at one end while we visited in there. But I wasn't comfortable until two weeks had passed. I still worried about her. Texas had been hit hard and her husband, David, was still working. They took lots of precautions and she mostly worked from home too, only had to go into the office periodically or to a meeting. Things wouldn't be good until we got a vaccine that helped everyone. I prayed for that day!

Blake and Gwen, her boys (Kingston, Zuma, and Apollo Rossdale), along with Todd and his family, remained in quarantine at Blake's ranch or lake house in Oklahoma (God's Country). It made sense because there was so much for creative people to do. Blake and Gwen continued to work on their music, and there was a little farming to be done. If they got tired of farm life, they could take a break at the house on the lake where there were water activities for the kids. The whole pandemic was hard on everyone, especially kids. They were lucky in that they were able to at least get out and do some fun and interesting things. Plus, Blake is still a big kid himself so he probably had more fun than any of them. I kept in touch through text, making only that one trip there to see him. Something was always happening.

They were able to do live and filmed performances, thanks to Todd. So that part was good. And it was announced that Blake, Gwen, and Trace Adkins would be performing in a drive-in concert that summer. The streamed concert would be shown at many drive-in theaters across the United States and Canada on July 25, 2020. Where there's a will, there's a way!

All during the pandemic, Blake continued to work on a new album, *Body Language,* with producer Scott Hendricks. It would become his twelfth studio album and not be released until May 21, 2021, but two singles would be released before the album. "Happy Anywhere" (Ross Copperman, Josh Osborne, Matt Jenkins), featuring Gwen Stefani, was released July 24, 2020, along with a video that featured many of the pictures Gwen had taken during their isolation. "Minimum Wage" (Nicolle Galyon, Jesse Frasure, Corey Crowder) was released January 15, 2021, and a performance video was seen on several television shows. As we say in Oklahoma, Blake didn't let any grass grow under him just because we were in the midst of a pandemic.

Looking back over the years you have known someone well is like taking another trip to a favorite vacation spot. It is the way I fall asleep every night. I pick someone special and start remembering some of my favorite times with them. I especially love doing that with my brothers, Ronnie Cash and Ricky Cash, who have both passed this life. Memories never grow old. And while writing this book, I journeyed again with family, friends, and Blake from the very beginning of his rise to fame. When I awoke, I wrote down my memories of our time with him. That went on for several years and I enjoyed every moment.

I had to do a little research and remember stories told to me by friends and family from his first dozen years, but after that, it was clear sailing. I remember well the first time I saw him perform on stage at the Music Palace in Ada, a chubby preteen with stars in his eyes. Following him as he gained an audience at the McSwain

Theatre and became increasingly more serious about a path in country music seems like yesterday sometimes. The day he came over to talk to Larry about wanting to actually go for a career as a singer/songwriter and Larry telling him he would help him if he finished high school first is crystal clear in my mind. Setting up a local concert to raise money for a Nashville showcase and making trips to Music City to attain a manager were simply the next steps in a long climb to the top of his field.

Making the big move, finding an apartment, and facing a future of hard work were fun at the time. When he became a little discouraged, I remember trying to keep his spirits up by reminding him that nothing worthwhile comes easy. After the years of boredom and watching *Jerry Springer* on a regular basis, finally came small opportunities to work with people in the business. Meeting Michael Kosser, writing with him, and being introduced to the legendary Bobby Braddock were big accomplishments. Working on getting a production deal and later a label were early goals. The first album, *Blake Shelton*, and having the first single, "Austin," go #1 for five straight weeks was a dream come true. Then came the fear that he was a one-hit wonder being dispelled when "The Baby" from his second album, *The Dreamer*, also flew to the top of the charts. Having one #1 hit from each of his first six albums made him a name in country music. When that sixth #1 started a string of seventeen consecutive chart-toppers that lasted over five years, he became a bona fide superstar. A little bobble after a rough patch in his personal life broke the string but gave him a unique song, "Savior's Shadow," and he was soon right back at the top. Being inducted into the Grand Ole Opry was a major highlight and he had us there to witness it firsthand. The awards started coming in 2010 and he began branching out.

After being picked up by Warner Bros., working with John Esposito, and signing on with Starstruck Management's Narvel Blackstock, things had really started popping. Scott Hendricks stepped in as producer and was at the helm of the string of consecutive #1s. The television guest spots, a Christmas album and television special, hosting a major award show, and being host as well as musical guest on *Saturday Night Live* were all epic moments. Writing the title track from the *Angry Birds* movie, raising lots of money for good causes, and climbing higher and higher with his career became overwhelming to me. I can't quite grasp how famous he has become. Signing on as a judge for *The Voice* was a stroke of genius. Being able to release a full album of just #1 hits—all of these moments were priceless.

And between all of this, there was still time for a growing fan club, time to go hunting and fishing, time to stay true to himself and make Oklahoma proud. He is still the same fun-loving, honest, talented, quick-witted guy he has always been.

To see where Blake is today amazes me. I had high hopes for him and always knew he would be successful, but he has exceeded my dreams for him. Often, I think back on his journey and realize that he has made great decisions along the way and that luck has been with him. I believe the fact that he is such a positive force has served him well. He possesses an old soul and a good heart. He is loyal to those who are loyal to him. What drew me to him in the first place, aside from his talent, was how he treated people. He would have been a great politician as he has such incredible charisma. When he is talking with you, his full attention is directed toward you. It never matters who you are—a celebrity, a child, a fan, a neighbor—you are treated with the same dignity and respect. If you could visit Tishomingo, where most of the residents didn't know him until he moved there just over a decade ago, I think you would hear the same thing. He's a good ol' boy who would sit down and have a beer with you if he had the time . . . which is a rare commodity these days. Blake is who he is when you see him on television. He doesn't mind trying something new or poking fun at himself. His fun-loving nature rubs off on everyone around him. There is nothing not to love about Blake Shelton. And it looks as though he has finally found his soulmate, Gwen Stefani.

It is only appropriate that Blake's journey began with "Ol' Red," when he first heard Hoyt Axton sing it to him on the bus right after his move to Nashville in 1994, popping up again as the third release off his debut album in 2002, quickly becoming his signature song, and finally in 2017 as a business venture with the Grand Ole Opry. As I wrap up these years, that droopy faced red dog is still hanging around Blake, having a new impact on his life.

I feel truly blessed that my family has had a front row seat at Blake's rise to fame. Larry, Debi, Patti, David, and I enjoy every success he has right along with Dorothy, Mike Shackleford, Endy, Mike Intrieri, Ryan, and Jace. And, I'm spiritual enough to believe Dick and Richie do too. I hope my brother Ronnie, who used to think Blake would forget all about us once he became famous, knows as well.

There is no telling what the future holds in store for Blake Shelton.

For a man who can truly be happy anywhere, there is no limit!

INDEX

Photo insert images appear in italics.